THE FIFTH SEASON

THE FIFTH SEASON

A Daughter-in-Law's Memoir of Caregiving

Lisa Ohlen Harris

Texas Tech University Press

Portions of this book first appeared in the following publications: "The Baptism" and "Air Hunger" in *Under the Sun*, "Autumn Sage" in *Ascent*, and "Comfort Food" in *Brevity*. "Her Choice," "April Fool," and "Thirty-One Days" first appeared in slightly different form as "Stranger in Blood" in *The Gettysburg Review*.

This book is typeset in Minion Pro. The paper used in this book meets the minimum requirements of ANSI/NISO Z39.48-1992 (R1997). ∞

Designed by Kasey McBeath
Cover illustration by Ashley Beck

Library of Congress Cataloging-in-Publication Data
Ohlen Harris, Lisa, 1963–
    The fifth season : a daughter-in-law's memoir of caregiving / Lisa Ohlen Harris.
        pages cm
    Summary: "A memoir of caregiving; illuminates the difficulties of and ethical questions surrounding end-of-life care in America"—Provided by publisher.
    Includes index.
    ISBN 978-0-89672-823-3 (hardback) — ISBN 978-0-89672-824-0 (e-book) 1. Terminal care—Moral and ethical aspects—United States. 2. Terminally ill—Family relationships. 3. Daughters-in-law—Family relationships. I. Title.
    R726.8.O44 2013
    362.17'5—dc23   2013022605

13 14 15 16 17 18 19 20 21 / 9 8 7 6 5 4 3 2 1

Texas Tech University Press
Box 41037 | Lubbock, Texas 79409-1037 USA
800.832.4042 | ttup@ttu.edu | www.ttupress.org

For Michelle, the other daughter-in-law

What I have to tell you must be explained
in a rather roundabout way.

Richard Bausch, "Letter to the Lady of the House"

Contents

Acknowledgments

This project has taken years to complete, and in that time many have added their fingerprints to the book you now hold in your hands. To my first critique partners, Karen Miedrich-Luo, Jill Kandel, and Nancy Nordenson—you three were with me for both the early writing of this account and the living of it. Thank you for editing my words and speaking into my life.

To the Rainier Writing Workshop, you dozens of writers who read and critiqued sections of this material year after year after year—how grateful I am to all of you! I must especially mention Gretchen Stahlman, Nancy Geyer, Stephen Corey, and Brenda Miller. Last and best, Judith Kitchen—your guidance is at once straight shooting and gentle; more than any other, you saw why this work was important and gave me the encouragement I needed to keep pushing through to the end.

My writing group here in Newberg is full of poets. Lynn Otto, Dave Mehler, Colleen Jefferey, and Keith Hansen—you are terrific readers and writers and friends, and I thank you for welcoming me into your fold. I'm also grateful to Carol Sherwood for her medical expertise and to Bettyann Henderson, who offered feedback through her tears, even as she was walking the last mile of this difficult road herself.

Because I have set down here a family history, I must acknowledge Jeanne's sons and grandchildren. To Scott and Jeff—after more than twenty years of being a Harris I have come to love you both as brothers. During the final, difficult years of your mom's life, I always knew that you loved me and you loved your mom and that there was no conflict between the two. I felt your support via e-mails and phone calls and visits, and I never once felt misunderstood by you. Thank you for allowing me to make our family story public.

To my daughters, Laurie, Ashley, Jessica, and Kayla—as I wrote this book I feared that my perspective would taint your memories of the G-Mom who adored you and gave and gave and always looked for ways to give some more. You were little girls in those years when G-Mom shared our home, and now you are young women. May you place your own memories between the lines of this book.

Genevieve, Justin, and Anna—you were an ocean away from us, but so close to your G-Mom's heart. She was proud of you and so delighted by every little thing she heard about your lives in France and in Hawaii. You three were a presence in our home, even when you were not physically in Texas. This book is written from an adult point of view, and I want you to understand the hard things I've written here, but this book holds my story, not yours. Remember your G-Mom through a child's eyes. Perhaps you will someday write your own books.

To Pam Wat, who came into our family for a brief season—you were a light on the path for us, Pam. Thank you for always speaking the truth.

To Michelle—you know me as no one else in this family does. You read this manuscript in its varying forms, and you offered thoughtful feedback and praise. Thank you for loving me, defending me, correcting me, and most of all thank you for listening to me and being my closest friend through all these years.

Todd Robert Harris. You knew I was a writer before I knew it myself, and over the years, you have given me not only your love, but also books and classes and computers and a room of my own. Thank you for always celebrating my writing life and for making my small accomplishments seem large. I love you.

THE FIFTH SEASON

This is a book about two very different women sharing a household and a family. It's about aging and caregiving and family obligations and resentment and hurt feelings and ethical convictions. Ultimately, this book chronicles a kind of reverse midwifery in which my mother-in-law and I held hands through her physical and mental decline, hospice care, and end of life.

Just after our tenth anniversary, Todd and I signed a mortgage together with his widowed mother on a home in a Philadelphia suburb. Jeanne selected pink carpet for her new in-law suite, while I decorated the main house in earth tones. She was not yet seventy. I was a young mother with three preschoolers. We now owned a much larger, newer home than Todd and I could have afforded on our own, and Jeanne lived in a house full of youth and life at an age when so many older adults are lonely. Despite small irritations, the arrangement seemed to work well. Jeanne shielded the girls from knowledge of her cigarette habit, smoking only in the bathroom of her in-law suite, with the door closed and the exhaust fan on high. She took the girls by turns on G-Mom dates; she joined a book club; she shopped and stocked our pantry; she paid more than her share when the heating bill was higher than expected. We felt so blessed, and we encouraged our friends to consider consolidating generations into one household. On our street alone we counted three other extended family households.

A fourth daughter was born just after Jeanne's first year with us, and we two women divided the responsibilities of caring for a newborn just as we'd navigated sharing a kitchen and holiday traditions—not always harmoniously, but we managed. Jeanne indulged the older girls as grandparents do—but most grandmothers aren't able to offer sweets and treats every day of the year. When I opened the pantry to put away my grocery purchases, there was no room. Even the floor was stacked with boxes of sugared cereals, packaged cookies, and the canned vegetables I'd always scorned. My children now asked for cinnamon sugar on their sliced apples and sips from Jeanne's Diet Coke. When one of the girls had a sore throat, I found Jeanne mixing powdered Jell-O into warm water as a soothing beverage. When I told her I wanted the girls to develop healthier habits, she insisted that the treats were only an expression of love and that the liquid Jell-O came recommended years ago by her own boys' pediatrician, who'd said sugar was the best thing for an ailing child.

One day Jeanne came home disgusted with her new physician, who had prescribed two medications for her irregular heartbeat. Her doctor back in Nebraska had never been concerned, so why should she trust this young guy? She later confided in me that the doctor had also spoken with her frankly about the harms of smoking, and at his suggestion she was considering hypnosis to break the habit. I raised my eyebrows but thought, why not? She'd tried everything else over the years. But Jeanne abandoned the idea of hypnosis. She kept on smoking, took the meds, and saw the new doctor only when absolutely necessary.

My husband's job changed, and we moved as an extended family from Pennsylvania to Jeanne's home state of Texas. We were celebrating our second holiday season in Texas—our fourth as an extended family sharing a home—when Jeanne got sick with what we thought was the same Christmas cold we'd been passing around the family. Only instead of getting better after a week, Jeanne grew increasingly short of breath. Her face was gray and she had no energy. She wound up hospitalized and was discharged into my care weak and discouraged, with new prescriptions and oxygen tanks and scheduled visits from home health nurses.

My life slowed to match hers as I entered the long season of caregiving, punctuated from time to time with frenzied trips to the hospital. My world contracted to the walls of our home and the labyrinths of emergency room hallways, where life stands still and it's hard to find a clock to record the passing time or windows to reveal the changing seasons. Jeanne and I formed an unlikely partnership, one that would hold fast as our journey took a turn into territory new to both of us.

My mother-in-law and I shared a household for seven years.

Jeanne's Christmas Cold

There was an old woman sat spinning
And that's the first beginning

Nursery rhyme

From home to hospital and back, I drive and fast-walk in a daze. I time myself in order to plan my hospital visits more efficiently. Twenty minutes' drive north on US 287 to downtown Fort Worth, seven minutes to walk from the parking garage through the hospital complex to the right building and take the elevator to the fifth floor, an hour for a visit, then twenty minutes home for a quick dinner and back to the hospital again with Todd and the girls before bedtime. Christmas is just two days away. The North Texas sun is bright, but the wind is bitter cold.

As I walk the hospital corridor to Jeanne's room, I look straight ahead and focus on the end of the hallway, to give privacy to the other patients. Still I see them through my peripheral vision: the thin woman with soft white hair cut too short, the toffee-skinned man who seems always to be coughing and choking—is this how death will come?

We've all had colds since school let out for the holidays, but Jeanne's hung on until she couldn't catch her breath, couldn't stop coughing. At the emergency room, we learned that her oxygen saturation was only at 65 percent, when normal oxygen sats are close to 100.

"How many years have you smoked?" the nurse asked.

"More than fifty," Jeanne answered.

Her hospital room looks out over blue neon lights outlining the rooftop of the adjacent children's hospital. The doctor can't say yet whether she'll come home by Christmas. The girls select ornaments from our tree to decorate Jeanne's hospital room, and they hang a wreath on the IV pole.

I'm driving home from the hospital when Jeff, Jeanne's second son, calls my cell phone. Jeff and Carolyn live with their seven-year-old daughter in Hawaii, where Jeff tells me that Carolyn has been admitted to the hospital with back pain and unexplained bruising; the initial blood tests are alarming. They say it might be something as serious as leukemia.

"When I left the hospital, there was a woman standing outside wailing," Jeff tells me. The woman's toddler had been killed and her husband gravely injured in a freak hiking accident. "I can't help feeling thankful," Jeff says, "because our situation is more hopeful."

Hope drains away when Jeff calls the next night to tell us that Carolyn has stage IV cancer, metastasized with tumors in her ovaries, lymph nodes, and bone marrow. Jeff sounds numb. His usually animated voice is flat and emotionless. They're thinking about a trip to Europe, Jeff says. At least they know she has three to six months left.

Carolyn is discharged two days before Christmas. Jeff drives her straight from the hospital to the church where their daughter, Genevieve, dresses in a special costume and holds a doll in swaddling clothes. Gen has waited since she was five to be Mary in the pageant; this is her big night.

"Let her have this last carefree Christmas," Jeff says when I ask why they haven't told Genevieve yet. "Everything is about to change for her. The world is about to get mean."

✧

Jeff sets his camera timer while Carolyn and Genevieve pose in the bright island sunshine. In a few days they will take Genevieve down to the beach to tell her. In January, the hospice will set up a hospital bed; nurses will come and go; three to six months will shrivel to less than two. The first week of February, Carolyn will be gone.

"Say Merry Christmas," Jeff calls out as brightly as he can and sprints to pose for this last family picture. Genevieve smiles widely and waits for the shutter to click.

✧

Back in Fort Worth it is Christmas Eve when the pulmonologist tells us Jeanne can come home. She'll need to use oxygen from now on, though in a few weeks, when she's stronger, Jeanne can wean herself off the tubes during the day and only wear the oxygen at night. He looks around her hospital room, touching the IV pole wreath as he speaks.

"If you keep smoking, I can guarantee you'll be back here for every holiday of the year. Imagine this room decorated for Valentine's, for St. Paddy's, for Easter." He discharges her with a prescription for antianxiety meds to get her through the withdrawal and an order for six weeks of visits from a home health nurse.

I help Jeanne dress and pack her few things. Jeanne coughs, then speaks quietly.

"It should be me, not Carolyn."

When she comes home to her in-law suite, Jeanne crumples the cigarette cartons hidden in her closet and asks me to get rid of them. She quits cold turkey—after all those years of failed attempts. For the first time in the four years we've shared a household, she's not locking herself in the bathroom to smoke. For the first time in the fifteen years I've known her, Jeanne doesn't reek.

On Christmas Day I hang three cloisonné hummingbirds—my gift to Jeanne—in her bay window, where she sits looking out past them to the chilled branches and yellowed, dry grass of winter.

The Baptism

Wade in the water
Wade in the water, children
Wade in the water
God's gonna trouble the water

Negro spiritual

Silk plants line the bathroom ledge in Jeanne's in-law suite. House-plants, like end tables and knickknacks, tend to gather dust, so a couple of times a year, I lower the dusty pots into the bathtub and dash water over them. I prefer real plants to fake ones, but the Texas sun is so hot on this side of the house that we've installed solar shades over all the windows, so neither heat nor plant-nourishing sunshine enters the bathroom. Silk plants are less trouble, and Jeanne needs things that require little of her these days. It is late March, three months since she was hospitalized at Christmas, and Jeanne has already been sick again twice with what Dr. Fletcher calls pulmonary exacerbations.

Jeanne is still a large woman, though illness and osteoporosis have changed her body from what it once was. She drops her robe on the floor, and I hold her hand from the toilet to the shower before bracing the plastic stool to keep it from sliding as she sits. My mother-in-law is naked and unashamed.

※

Todd and I sat on the rocky Oregon shoreline as waves hit the rocks beneath us and crashed into mist. He twisted his new ring and held his left hand to mine, palm to palm.

"Twenty-two hours now," he said. "You've been my wife for almost an entire day."

Out beyond the breakers, the waters swarmed with living creatures. A whale surfaced, submerged, then surfaced again: the ancient leviathan. We walked back along the upper beach, where firm damp sand divided itself from dry land. Kelp, mussel, sandpiper, we named them.

Evening came, then morning, and we had been married for two days.

I point the handheld nozzle so the water flows over Jeanne's hands. She tells me when the temperature is just right, and we begin.

As I hold up her arm to soap the armpit, I ask about the scar across her belly. Kidney stones. Above the scar her breasts are small, but they sag just the same. She insisted on breastfeeding her babies in the 1960s, when formula feeding was at an all-time high in the United States.

I lift one of her breasts with my left hand to draw the soapy rag under it. "Mom, is this okay?"

"Oh, yes," she says. "That helps so much, dear."

It is comfortable for both of us, this intimacy. As I wash her most private areas, as I see each of her scars, I think: With this body she bore three sons.

The minister held our firstborn before the assembly. "I baptize you in the name of the Father and of the Son and of the Holy Spirit." Water fell from his cupped hand onto our child's head, drops rolling off her fine hair and onto the minister's arm.

In the pouring of baptismal waters, believers see a picture of sacrificial blood, of parting seas, of Christ's own baptism, of the pouring out of the Holy Spirit on the Day of Pentecost. A world of meaning was played out in droplets on our sleeping baby's brow. She was christened Laurie Elisabeth Harris.

We gave our child a first and middle name after my best friend and myself. I was named for both my grandmothers. Todd and I liked the thought of giving our fresh newborn names that already carried a wealth of love and significance: Laurie Elisabeth. Jeanne said it was a lovely name, full of meaning. In later years, she would reveal her hurt that we spelled Elisabeth without the traditional *z*. By choosing the *s*, which places my lifelong nickname, Lisa, at the center of the longer name, she was certain that we had intentionally excluded her own mother, another Elizabeth.

We chose our baby's name months before she was born. In all those happy phone calls to Todd's parents—*the baby kicks so hard now; the ultrasound showed it's a girl; do you like the name we've picked out?*—Jeanne never gave us a chance, never reminded us that there was another Elizabeth in the family.

Like the first man and the first woman in Genesis, our union brought forth a child. And like that first child of Genesis, our baby was born into thorns and curses and enmity.

To this day, my eldest daughter, this youngest Elisabeth, is the one my mother-in-law presses and humiliates again and again, while accepting and loving my other daughters, so that even the girls themselves see the difference and wonder about it. I wonder, too: is it my fault, because I chose *s* instead of *z*?

There were currents I didn't see or feel in those early years. My actions carried significance beyond what I understood.

Jeanne tilts her head back and closes her eyes as I shampoo her hair. I massage her scalp, take my time. After rinsing, she holds the shower head pointed at her chest and enjoys the cascading warmth while I close the shampoo, wring out the washrag, and line the bathroom chair with dry towels. I turn off the water and help her from the shower stool to the bathroom chair. I apply lotion while her skin is still moist from the shower. The scent of lavender on her skin reminds me of baby powder.

One summer day when our second daughter, Ashley, was a year old, we had friends over to play in our wading pool. While the other mother changed her child's diaper, I ran a hose in through the kitchen window then went inside to attach it to the faucet so that I could fill the pool with warm water. Once I had the hose attached, I came back outside and reached in through the window to adjust the temperature.

When I turned to the pool, Ashley's head was under the water, her body folded over the side, bottom sticking up in the air the same way it did when she slept. She wiggled. She kicked. She couldn't lift her head out of the water. I took four quick steps over to my child, grasped her wiggling hips, and plucked Ashley out.

If I'd run to the back of the house for towels instead of glancing at the pool, it might have been too late.

❖

The lotion softens her skin, and I can tell by feel where I haven't yet applied it. I pull my hands gently over her sagging calves and down to her bruised ankles. Her legs and arms are spotted with cuts and bruises these days. Her skin tears so easily that even brushing against a footstool results in an open wound that takes weeks to heal. To avoid infection and to offer comfort, I bandage the oozing wounds. I dress them with gauze and a stretchy wrap, because adhesive bandages tear her skin.

When Jeanne feels better in a few weeks, when she recovers from this exacerbation and before the next ailment strikes, I will not feel as compassionate. We've begun a cycle that will repeat itself for the rest of Jeanne's life—illness or injury knocks her out almost completely, and I am there to take care of her. When she is most weak, she doesn't criticize me or Todd or the girls. Jeanne and I are the closest of friends. Then she will slowly gain strength until she feels better—never as good as she wishes she felt—and she will reach again for the independence her poor health has stripped from her. Perhaps it is her disloyal body she means to flagellate and not me at all.

Sometimes, I'm ashamed to say it, I wish for her to remain at the lowest point so that she won't rise up again and hurt me or Laurie. I hate to feel content only when Jeanne is at her worst. But I am. It is easier for me—sweeter between us—when she is most frail. She thinks the burden is in the caregiving; she's apologetic when I become her nurse, her confidante and friend.

"Lisa, maybe you should put me in a nursing home."

I wipe my hands on a towel and sit up on the edge of the tub so I can look into her eyes.

"No, Mom," I say. Her eyes tear and her face relaxes. "We'll do fine, Mom. We want you home with us." And I mean it, at this moment, with all my heart.

She's told me many times—no chemo if it's cancer, no ventilator if it's her lungs. No intervention. She wants to die at home.

"We will never send you to a nursing home."

"Thank you for saying so," she says. "I just needed to hear it again today."

My mother-in-law has already lost her vital years. In this latter-day baptism, Jeanne feels the life going out of her. Pneumonia fills her lungs with fluid, and like a child with her head caught underwater, she needs me to grab on and help.

Some days the caregiving feels like a privilege. Other days I wonder if it will be too heavy to bear when she is frail and always frailer, when the waters surround her and she can't pull herself back out. I wonder whether I can keep my promise to her when the end comes. My mother-in-law is taller and heavier than I am. I don't think I can lift her, if it comes to that. I have four young children who need my care. Jeanne is not my mother. Sometimes I wonder why I'm the one.

❖

When Laurie was five and Ashley was two, we visited the zoo. The girls laughed wildly, gripping the molded manes of the carousel creatures—one of them on a pink unicorn and the other on a gold lion. Todd stood between them, pointing out which direction to wave to Mommy and Baby Jessa each time the carousel brought them around.

I clicked my nursing bra closed and lowered Jessica into the umbrella stroller. I adjusted the detachable sun shade so she wouldn't get burned.

The girls came running up to me, Todd striding behind them. "The monkey house next, Mama—come on!"

Ashley was just eighteen months old when Jessica was born. I wore nursing bras for nearly four years in a row. Many times during those years, I wondered if I would always be there on the sidelines, watching Todd with the older girls while I nursed another baby, and yet another.

We lived far from family and didn't have the money for a babysitter, so I had my three preschoolers with me full time. I used two grocery carts—one for kids, one for groceries. A woman can't push two grocery carts for long before ramming into a display or losing control of one of them. So I learned to push one cart with my left hand and with the right hand pull the other.

Laurie started first grade the year her G-Mom moved in with us. Jeanne cooked and drove and babysat in those first years sharing a household. Jessica was out of diapers, and I was off the sidelines and into the action for the first time since I'd quit working to have Laurie. Then a surprise pregnancy brought us a fourth daughter, born cesarean section like all the rest. As the nurses suctioned out Kayla's lungs and I heard her first cry, my obstetrician asked, "No more babies, right? Are you sure you want the tubal ligation? Absolutely sure?"

"Snip away!" I told him. I could almost see the light at the end of the tunnel.

Kayla is three now. I threw the nursing bras away years ago, and the diaper money has long been reallocated to our growing grocery budget. I still use two carts with the push-one-pull-one method when I make a major grocery shopping trip for our extended family of seven.

I am learning to use the push-one-pull-one skill when I take Jeanne to the ER and she's too short of breath to walk on her own. I push her in the wheelchair and pull the wheeled oxygen tank along behind us. Getting a wheelchair through a door or down a curb is surprisingly like maneuvering a stroller. Parenting prepared me for this new season of caregiving.

Todd took the girls camping a few weeks ago. I stayed home with Jeanne, who has been recovering from an exacerbation. When he called me on the cell phone, I heard the girls in the background, laughing and breathless, chasing imaginary lions and unicorns around and around the campsite. Even without a baby to watch after, I'm still on the sidelines, still nursing the one who needs me.

That night, alone in our king-sized bed, I wept.

✥

I help Jeanne into a fresh gown and robe, and I set the lotion back on the shelf for next time. The hot air from the blow dryer dissipates the steam from the bathroom mirror. I see Todd's hairline in hers as I brush and lift and blow, the same gentle widow's peak that is mirrored on each member of my family. This is the hairline I saw on each fuzzled newborn—the hairline that assured me they'd brought the right baby.

She has a small mole on the back of her left ear. Todd has a mole on the back of his right ear, a mirror-image genetic reflection of his mother's. I still remember the first time I noticed it on him. I sat in the backseat of a friend's car while he sat in the passenger's seat ahead of me. His hair curled over his collar in the back, pushed behind his ears on the sides. We'd been dating only a short time, but already we talked of marriage. In that small spot of pigment I saw foreshadowed other secret scars and blemishes to be revealed over many years of lovemaking. Isn't romantic love like that? With shining eyes I saw a world of hope and promise—yes, in an ear mole. Silly girl. But our union has been sweet. I love all his blemishes and all his scars. I suppose that dreamy-eyed girl in the backseat did see the future. Not all the details, though. If she had foreseen that she would one day know her mother-in-law's blemishes and scars as well as her husband's, would she have bolted from the car that night?

We dream and imagine. We make solemn vows at baptisms and weddings. But we cannot see the future. We don't understand the promises embedded in our actions until years after we've made them.

In caring for my mother-in-law, I reach to the past, to my backseat hopes for this man, to my months and years as a young mother giving care to a newborn—further back even, to when I was a babe myself, and somewhere in the Midwest a woman with a mole behind her ear nursed her own baby boy. I reach for that past and I join it with the present.

"There you go, Mom."

I unplug the blow dryer, slip the brush back into the drawer. The damp towels are now in a heap for me to carry out to the laundry room.

"You know, Lisa, you could save yourself a lot of trouble."

"How's that?"

"If you could just backtrack about sixteen years and not marry into this mess."

I married *Todd,* promising to stay with *him* till death separates us. I did not marry his mother. My religious commitments discourage divorce but would sanction it in grim circumstances. I have never felt my marriage was grim. But I have regretted that when she became a widow I invited and insisted she move to be with us, years ago, when she was well and strong. For now, without making holy promises, I have nonetheless entered into a covenant of care with her that will not easily be broken.

We make our marriage vows in a cloud of smiles and joy and anticipation. For richer, for poorer—with no concept of either extreme. In sickness and in health—not knowing how a head injury or sudden cancer could twist a wealth of promises into hardship. With a kiss, two lives are joined like an unbroken circle. Till death separates us.

I suspect that I will be with my mother-in-law until death separates her from me. This, too, is a holy union. A new creation has happened here—the formation of a family tie where blood does not bind. Like our first parents, cast out of paradise, I step on thorns and thistles. I wish for a way out—anything, anything but death to release me from this. But it is too late. I remember. I lament. I resent. I love.

Jeanne reaches out to squeeze my hand. And now, she says she wants to rest, to sleep.

Once I've helped her into bed, I gather the towels. I leave the bedroom door open, like I did for my newborn babies. While she sleeps, I will tiptoe in from time to time to peek and see whether she's okay, as I did with my little ones, as she did when my husband was a baby. Each time I check on her my heart will speed up, anxiety rising, until I see she is still breathing.

Air Hunger

I had a little pony
His name was Dapple-Gray
I lent him to a lady
To ride a mile away

Nursery rhyme

Four months after Jeanne's Christmas hospitalization, a brochure arrives for a family camp nestled in the mountains outside of Colorado Springs. Evergreens all up and down the mountains, trails wandering off through the trees, cabins with decks for reading and relaxing. Seven days of activities for the kids and camp staff doing the cooking and cleaning. No driving the freeways or calling Jeanne's doctors or gritting my teeth so I don't snap at her. At family camp we would be hiking, rappelling, riding horses, looking out over wild vistas.

Todd's eldest brother, Scott, is flying back from France with his family this summer and wants us to spend a week together at family camp. They'll fly into Dallas–Fort Worth and drive up to Colorado with us, then come for a longer visit with Jeanne afterward. But I worry that Jeanne will need help while we're gone. She still drives—except for the freeways—but she needs my help more and more for so many of the small things that make up a day. She can't get the lid off a jam jar to make herself a sandwich. I fix her oxygen tubing when it gets loose. On mornings when Jeanne wakes short of breath and coughing blood-tinged sputum, I drive her twenty minutes up the freeway to the emergency room. She's had two serious respiratory infections in the four months since Christmas. She hates wearing the oxygen at home and refuses to wear it in public. Sometimes her oxygen level drops and she can't think straight. Jeanne gulps for breath—her doctor calls it "air hunger"—and at these times I think for both of us, always pretending that she is still the one making the decisions, that she's still thinking things through.

Each time Jeanne is hospitalized, we visit her, carry in Diet Coke and warm socks, whatever she needs. When she's discharged, Todd makes a trip to the pharmacy to fill prescriptions while I help her change into a nightgown and snip the plastic ID band off her wrist. She'll say how good it feels to be back in her own bed—"Oh, Lisa. There's something else." The blouse she wore to the hospital got stained—she hates to ask me to do so much, but it's her favorite blouse. I tell her I'll treat it and soak it right away, try to get the stains out. All I want is for her to go to sleep so I can lock myself in the bathroom and take a hot bath.

"One more thing, dear," she'll say. "Thank you so much for all this. I know it's not easy for you."

"I'm glad to do it, Mom," I'll say. But I'm not telling the truth. I don't want to be her best friend, her caregiver. I am tight and weary and desperate for time away. I, too, have air hunger.

✧

"Mom, what does *nuclear family* mean?" eight-year-old Ashley asks. We're folding laundry together, Ashley matching the socks while I sort clean school uniform blouses according to size.

"A nuclear family is the parents and children," I say.

"That's what I thought," Ashley says. "But when I told G-Mom we were learning about families in school, she told me a nuclear family sometimes includes the grandma."

"What?"

"Yeah. She said our nuclear family in this house is Mommy and Daddy and G-Mom and all the sisters."

"Did you tell her that's not what your teacher says?"

Ashley shrugs. "I just wanted to know for sure."

My laid-back Ashley is such a sweet little peacekeeper. I get riled up enough for the both of us. Jeanne has redefined *nuclear family* to squeeze herself right on in. No wonder her feelings get hurt when we want to go on vacation without her.

�֍

"Scott says we need to make a deposit soon if we're going to family camp," Todd says from the computer. We're both upstairs in the loft, where we have privacy from Jeanne so long as we keep our voices low.

"I don't see how we can leave your mom for an entire week," I say.

Todd leaves the computer and comes to sit beside me. "You can't let yourself feel guilty about taking a one-week vacation once a year."

I feel plenty guilty. When we traveled to New Mexico two summers ago, we called Jeanne the first night from Amarillo, her hometown in the Texas Panhandle. But we didn't call again, not from Santa Fe or Los Alamos or Albuquerque. We didn't call her again until five days later, when we decided to drive straight through from Roswell and arrive home earlier than intended. Jeanne spoke tersely that she'd been worried sick. When I asked why she didn't call one of our cell numbers to check on us, she said she assumed if we'd wanted to talk to her, *we* would have made the call.

The next vacation, I called her every day. But the family camp brochure says we won't have cell phone coverage at camp, and even if I could call her every day I know Jeanne well enough to know there will be some other unspoken expectation I'm sure to miss.

"What about it, Lisa? Let's do this family camp thing."

"She'll resent us," I say. "A week of family vacation isn't worth the cost." You'd think I'm the daughter and Todd the son-in-law.

"Sweetie, we can't sit around waiting for her to die before we take another vacation," Todd says. And I know he's right. We've got to make memories with our four girls while they're still living at home.

"We can't leave Jeanne alone for a week," I say. "Not when we can't even call to check in on her."

"What about Uncle Harry?" Todd asks. "I'll bet he'd love to come."

It's a wonderful idea. Jeanne will be so excited to have her brother and his wife come. This is the perfect solution—a treat for her and a vacation for us. Perfect, and yet . . .

"I wouldn't want to get her hopes up if Harry's busy that week," I say.

"Let me call and make sure he's willing," Todd says. "Then we'll tell Mom."

I take a deep breath, almost a sigh. Jeanne will be so happy. This is the perfect solution—if Harry says yes.

✿

"Glad to help," Harry says. "Tell Sis we're looking forward to it." But Jeanne isn't pleased.

"Do you think I need a *babysitter*?"

"Oh, no, Mom, it's not like that."

"You don't think I can function on my own?"

What is "function" anyway? She wipes herself. She takes a shower. Because of an arm injury a couple of years ago she can't fix her own hair, so I do that for her. I open the pill bottles when a childproof lid is too much for her arthritis. I do her laundry. I reach things down and plug things in; I untangle and troubleshoot and repair. I cancel play dates and book club meetings when she's sick and needs me to stay home. I preface any social plans with, "If nothing comes up with my mother-in-law."

Jeanne used to be a caseworker for the community council on aging. "Caregivers need time for themselves, too," she told her clients. "It's nothing to feel guilty about." That younger Jeanne, the compassionate social worker, would have told me I had to get away. But this weaker Jeanne, insecure, with so much stripped away, does not want to think of herself as dependent.

✿

The girls have gone to bed and I join Todd on the couch in the loft. He puts his arm around me and I tuck my feet up and curl close to his side.

"I tried to talk with Mom about family camp," he says. "I even asked her how she felt about Harry and Cathy coming. She said 'It's fine' and turned on her TV to some ice skating thing."

"She hates the whole plan," I say. "I feel rotten. I thought she would love to see Harry and Cathy. I guess I should have asked her first—I really thought we were doing the right thing."

"Well, the plan is made," Todd says. "Harry and Cathy are coming here and we're going to Colorado."

I'm so much closer to Jeanne than Todd is. When I remember how our relationship started—what her expectations were, and mine—it seems inconceivable that things would turn out like this, that I would bond with Jeanne and want her to come live with us.

Todd is the youngest of three brothers and the only introvert in a family of extroverts. But Todd was the first son to marry, and Jeanne saw me as the answer to her longings for a daughter. She expected me to be, as a newlywed, the kind of best friend daughter-in-law I am to her now. I did not live up to her expectations in those first months, even years, but I don't remember being troubled. No guilt back in those newlywed days.

I made Todd answer the phone on weekends, and if it was Jeanne, I'd quickly get myself elbow deep in dishwater or go into the bathroom and turn on the fan. It's not that I disliked her. At twenty-eight, I was adjusting to being someone's wife instead of a single woman on my own. I had a new job with a senior editor who found so many errors in my work that I despaired of earning her professional trust. The new expectations and changing roles were plenty for me without adding an intimacy with my mother-in-law. I kept an emotional distance from Todd's parents. I suppose I hoped that Jeanne's fervor to be close to me would, in time, cool.

❖

The dining hall stretches along one side of the wide sward at the center of camp. Along two sides of the hall are picture windows, red hummingbird feeders centered outside each.

I sit in the tree swing, reading slowly and dreaming between paragraphs. Under one of the windows, the camp photographer tries to get a shot of the hummingbirds from below. He bends at the waist then twists sideways to angle the camera up.

A hummingbird falls to the feeder like a raindrop, hovers for a moment, then that bird is gone and another is in its place. They look identical, like clones of one another, each compact body aloft in a wingless blur.

The photographer tilts and rolls his upper body, trying to find the right angle. He focuses the lens and waits for a hummingbird to come into the viewfinder and then, seeing a bird out of the corner of his eye, he ducks and pans the camera to catch only the blur of wings or tail feathers. He lowers the camera and laughs.

Rain speckles my book, so I step inside the dining hall until the shower passes. The picture windows frame the mountains, each hummingbird feeder suspended against the rugged backdrop.

My sister-in-law Michelle carries a box of dominoes from the game cupboard. "Let's play Mexican Train," she says. We sit at a table near the windows. The rain shower has already passed. Michelle dumps out the dominoes, and I help her flip them upside down.

"There's Laurie," Michelle says as we clack dominoes into position. I look out the window to see what my eleven-year-old is up to. Just this morning Laurie coaxed a chipmunk out of its burrow by holding her finger at the top of the opening and laying a peanut down just outside the hole. As the chipmunk emerged to sniff at the offering, Laurie's finger brushed its head lightly, then again, until she was stroking a wild chipmunk and feeding it peanuts from her hand.

Now Laurie stands still and tall under the hummingbird feeder, balancing on a wooden high chair borrowed from the dining hall. As the birds pulse above her, Laurie reaches upward, her hand and arm trembling slightly. The birds dance in and out, hovering for seconds to feed above Laurie's hand—just out of reach—and then darting off again.

"The photographer told Laurie that if she's patient and holds her finger under the feeder, a hummingbird will light on it," Michelle says, clicking dominoes as she flips and mixes them for the game.

"He shouldn't mess with her like that," I say.

"No—I think it's true. If she's patient."

The feeder's red base and faux yellow flowers are bright against the gray sky. Laurie reaches above her head.

"Look, she's going to scare them," Michelle says.

Three hummingbirds hover, their wings whirring as they feed on the sugar water. Laurie extends her forefinger, but she doesn't wait patiently for the birds to become accustomed to her presence. She lifts her hand closer and closer to the underbelly of the nearest hummingbird, raises her hand until she touches the bird's suspended feet; the hummingbird relaxes and stops beating its wings. For half a minute—a long time in the life of a hummingbird—the small creature stands on Laurie's hand and drinks sugar water.

Adjacent to the dining hall is a small shop offering sweatshirts, sunscreen, and a few knickknacks and books. The shop is open at all hours, and campers list purchases on a sheet of paper in order to settle up the last day of camp. Blown-glass hummingbirds hang at varying heights in front of a lighted mirror. I select one for Jeanne and record its price at the counter. I cushion the delicate beak and wings with the only padding material I can find in our cabin—a clean pair of pink cotton underpants—and I tuck my parcel into the glove compartment of our car for the ten-hour drive back home to North Texas. Jeanne loves hummingbirds. Maybe this gift will soften her hard feelings and bring harmony between us.

❁

Jeanne is a verbal processor. To understand what's happening in her life, to make a decision, she must talk things through. When I'm not away on vacation, I join Jeanne in her sitting room for a visit every morning. She'll tell me how she slept and we'll talk through any plans for the day. I sip my coffee while Jeanne drinks her first Diet Coke. She turns on her nebulizer and breathes in the vaporized medication to open her airways; often Jeanne will switch the nebulizer off and mute the television when she thinks of one more thing she wants to tell me. Jeanne shows her love by opening her heart to me and putting words on what she finds there. I demonstrate my love by sitting still for thirty minutes each morning when I'd rather be getting things done around the house. Jeanne tells me I know her better than anyone else alive, that I'm her best friend.

She has other friends here in Fort Worth, of course, but there's not the same history she had with folks back in Nebraska and Indiana, where she built a life in her prime. Friends in Hastings knew Jeanne as a leader at the YWCA and at church, a facilitator of grief support groups. The phone would ring and her best friend Nancy would be on the line, telling Jeanne to go outside and look up because the cranes were flying over. Nancy lived a few miles north of Jeanne; in the fall, Nancy heard the cranes first and called Jeanne. When the migration reversed in spring, Jeanne would be the one to hear the cranes first and give Nancy a call.

"Oh, how I miss the Sandhill cranes," Jeanne will say. "So majestic on the Platte River." And I know she also misses Nancy, who died of breast cancer the year after Laurie was born. Jeanne and I have a history. I know her for who she was years ago. When the Canada geese fly overhead I throw open a window and call for Jeanne to come.

Each year on my birthday, Jeanne writes me a letter telling me the qualities she sees in me and how she admires these things. I would like to say I treasure these notes of affirmation, but honestly they embarrass me. Jeanne's articulate intimacy makes me face my own difficulty verbalizing affection. On her birthday in early April, I bake her favorite coconut cake. I drive her south on US 287 to look at the bluebonnets. For supper I broil pork chops because she loves them so. Am I motivated by love or by duty—or is there even a difference between the two? My very favorite moments with Jeanne are when we sit together in silence, because we have known one another so long and so well there's no need for talk.

❖

Ends up Jeanne had a blast while we were in Colorado. Harry drove, and they went everywhere. Out to dinner every night, she tells me, and they had such fun seeing the Fort Worth stockyards one day and driving along the Trinity River the next. Harry took the car for an oil change, bless his heart. She isn't angry at me for leaving. She's not hurt.

I hang the glass bird from a thin piece of elastic, where it bobs and hovers near its cloisonné counterparts in the bay window over Jeanne's desk. The hummingbird is more than a pretty thing to Jeanne. It's evidence that I didn't forget about her when we were off on vacation at a "family" camp that didn't include her.

A small package arrives in the mail—a CD from the camp photographer. I snuggle with Laurie on the couch and push the disk into my laptop. When we come to the hummingbirds, Laurie wraps herself in the memory. She tells how she reached up, how she broke into their world. She tells of touching the hummingbird's breast as it drank. Laurie's long legs rest over my knees, which is the closest she can come these days to sitting on my lap. I don't rush the moment by shifting to a more comfortable position. Ever since Carolyn died, leaving Genevieve without a mother, I've tried to slow myself down, to touch and hold while I can.

"Mama," Laurie says to me, her voice reverent, "that hummingbird was as soft as cotton."

Map of Dallas

Bessy kept the garden gate
And Mary kept the pantry
Bessy always had to wait
While Mary lived in plenty

Nursery rhyme

The day after we've returned from family camp, Harry tells us he took Jeanne's car for the oil change after she commented that the plastic chairs in the service area's waiting room were hard on her back.

"You kids should see about her car from now on," Harry says.

"We can do that," Todd agrees.

I feel the edge of a headache. If Todd sees about Jeanne's car then I'll resent that he's sitting at the service area reading a book with his feet up while I'm home seeing about the kids and his mom. I know I should have compassion for Jeanne, but we've got four small children, and I already feel like I do more for Jeanne than I do for them.

Harry adds that it would be good if we could keep her gas tank full, too, especially in the hot weather when it's hardest for her to stand in the heat and fill the tank. The hot part of the year in North Texas lasts about six months.

"Oh, and she told me about the yearly emissions inspection," Harry goes on. "That's another thing. Just get her registration out of her glove box and have the inspection done for her, will you?" Harry continues, "Sis needs more help these days. I know it often takes someone from the outside to really see the decline."

I can't say it out loud, but I wish there were more decline. I wish she would have to give up driving altogether.

"I love my sis," Harry says. "Thanks for all you do. And one more thing. She seems confused at times—have you thought about setting up the pills for her?"

Two Saturdays a month Jeanne fills her pillboxes with the various pills she takes morning and evening. After her first hospitalization last Christmas, when she was so worn out during the long recovery, I offered to organize the pills. She grew pouty and asked me if I trusted her. For days she was tightlipped and silent when I entered the room. No way. I won't touch the pills. She's not my mother, and even after all these years I can't fight with her and know she still loves me. I avoid conflict as much as I can. I'll fill her gas tank.

Fifteen years ago—two weeks after our wedding—Todd and I drove from Oregon to Philadelphia and moved into a tiny second-floor apartment. Our landlord, Sam, was a born-again Christian, and our apartment had been his first home when he was a newlywed himself. The downstairs neighbor had rented from Sam for nearly thirty years and was old enough to be Sam's own mother.

"Rose is alone," he said. "She comes across ornery, but I care about her. Just keep an eye out, would you?" Why Sam cared, I wasn't sure. Rose stuck her head out the door to criticize our heavy footsteps on her ceiling and to tell us we'd left a window open and didn't we know it was a bad neighborhood? I dreaded seeing her. When I came home from work, I walked from the train with my house key positioned for speedy entry. If I saw her curtains move and heard the deadbolt unlocking, I moved faster, shut the door behind me, and tried to keep my footsteps light as I dashed up the stairs.

One afternoon we came home from the grocery store to find Rose knocking frantically on the *inside* of her door. It was too strange.

"Help me, please. Someone help me."

"Rose, what's wrong?"

"Somebody? My door is broken. It won't open, won't open."

"Rose, the door is locked. Turn the bolt and I can open it from outside."

Her words became more confused.

"Help where see no lock. Sick 'neath sweater."

Todd went upstairs to call the landlord, who kept a spare key. We were young, in our twenties, and had no idea what might be wrong. I talked to Rose through the door, telling her about my day, the flowers in the neighbor's garden, the cat across the street. She leaned against the door, calmer, but her words still jumbled when she spoke.

By the time our landlord arrived and opened the door, Rose had gone to the back of the apartment. Sam told me to go in first, and he asked Todd to stay with him while I checked. Rose stood by her bed, naked with her arms caught up in her sweatshirt halfway over her head.

"Stuck hot in," she whimpered. Her breasts lay nearly flat against her white belly.

"I'm here, Rose. I'll help you."

"Hot too and sleep." Rose glided down the side of the bed to the floor. I called down the hall that she had fallen and I needed help.

"Do you have clothes on her?"

"Not yet. She fell."

"Get her decent first."

Somehow I managed to help Rose get the sweatshirt back on while she whispered nonsense in my ear. The men came back and made a chair with their arms, to carry Rose out to the car.

"Rose, I'll take you to my place," Sam said in a bright voice as he buckled her in. He clicked down the lock and shut the door. "Hospital, actually," he told us. "The last time she was there she nearly died. Swore she would never go back—she's sure she'll die if she does." He stepped back into the house to grab a paper grocery sack and dump all her prescription medicine bottles into it. I was amazed. I would never have thought to do that—not back then.

Years of history between Sam and Rose packed meaning into every word and motion between them. Todd and I saw only the ornery old woman alone downstairs, a prudish caution, the averting of eyes, the white lie for her own good.

She was out of the hospital in a few days, courteous and cranky by turns as usual. I began to feel a strange fondness for Rose and found myself relieved to see the quick pull of her white hand on the curtain as I came up the walk.

❖

I tell Todd I'd like him to stay home with his mom and the girls while I take Jeanne's car for the emissions inspection. At least if I do it myself I resent my mother-in-law and not my husband.

First I need to make sure I have her registration in hand, but Jeanne's glove box is crammed with junk, just like anyone else's, and I can't find the registration. She insists it's there.

"Bring it all in, dear, and I'll sort through," she says. Crunched papers from tire repairs, wrapped drinking straws, the map of Dallas she bought the week we moved to Fort Worth—before she decided the freeways were too much for her. Her cigarette lighter, asthma inhaler, mints, and cologne. The registration is tucked into a stack of fast-food napkins. Underneath it all I find a yellowed plastic knife with dried gunk in the serrations. Maybe she pitched it in there along with the extra napkins from a fast food stop—absentmindedly, the same way I sometimes put dishtowels in the fridge. Maybe the plastic knife is yellowed because it's been in there since before she stopped smoking. The car itself still reeks even though it's been eight months now since she was hospitalized and quit cold turkey.

❖

When Todd and I lived in the apartment above Rose's in Philly, Jeanne was caring for her own aging mother—long distance. Jeanne's mom still lived in Amarillo, ten hours from Jeanne's home in Hastings, Nebraska. Twice a month, Jeanne would prepare a few days' worth of meals for her husband and stack them neatly in the fridge, labeled with day/meal/heating instructions, and she'd drive from Nebraska to Texas. It was a ten-hour trip, and she'd make it in one long drive fueled by cigarettes, a cooler of Diet Coke, and audiobooks. Eventually Jeanne's mother couldn't live on her own and they moved her to Hastings and hired full-time caregivers.

"Mother waited too long," Jeanne always says. "She waited until she *had* to move closer to me—and by the time she did, it was too late for her to make a new life for herself in Hastings. I was her social life until the day she died." That's why Jeanne moved in with Todd and me soon after her husband died but before she "needed to." We knew, when we signed that mortgage together, that Jeanne would eventually grow frail and that we would care for her when she did.

As her belongings traveled across the country in a moving truck, Jeanne drove herself from Hastings to Philadelphia. No big deal. Driving across the country alone was easy for Jeanne, back then.

Our friends in Pennsylvania were so impressed. Shocked that she was driving herself. Nearly everyone we knew in Pennsylvania had relatives living close—for many of them the world beyond Lancaster County was wide and foreign. I loved that Jeanne's reputation—an independent, able woman—preceded her. When she arrived, she stood tall, like a queen. The first Sunday she came to church with us to meet our friends, Jeanne dressed like a successful artist. Classy black pumps lifted her to an easy five-foot-ten. She wore a bold pendant and dangly earrings with her long black knit dress. Over her shoulders she draped the alpaca shawl purchased when she traveled alone to Colombia to join Scott and Michelle in Bogota and meet her grandson. As our friends greeted Jeanne, I knew they'd be thinking, *What a woman—she drove halfway across the country on her own.* I felt proud of her in every way that day. Even how she masked the cigarette smoke with breath mints and a spritz of spunky perfume.

Now, five years later, she barely functions in the car. She's the slow old lady in the right-hand lane. She parks in a handicapped spot and grabs onto the frame of the car to pull herself up and out. She shops only at stores that provide an electric cart with an attached basket, because walking leaves her out of breath. When we shop together, I push a big cart while she buzzes off down the aisles in the electric one. She piles up the tiny basket like a geometry problem. The carton of Diet Coke fits upright in a corner of the basket, conserving space. A box of crackers slides in beside the Coke carton, and a bag of oranges holds them in place. Cream-filled cupcakes, sugar cereal for the kids, all sorts of hydrogenated treats to fill in the spaces, the lightweight stuff balanced on top until her basket becomes a tower that reaches to the sky.

Always a compulsive shopper, Jeanne still loves spending money. When I shop with her, I see the piled cart and I remember cartons of disposable diapers under Laurie's crib in Philly—outgrown before we could use them all. The darling baby dresses, bought on sale and sent from Nebraska to Philadelphia in large boxes, crowding the closet until I purged and donated armfuls of outfits that still had the tags on. The overpacked electric cart reminds me of all this—the cans and cartons layered in her basket tell who she is and was—just like the contents of her glove box do. When she can't fit any more in, she crams things beside her on the seat and between her feet on the base of the cart. Other shoppers comment, even tease, about how full she manages to get her basket.

"We have seven people at our house," she says with a grin. "This stuff will last us about an hour." I'm proud of her verve. And embarrassed that she buys so much. I'm thankful that when we shop together she always picks up the tab. And frustrated there's so much waste. Buy the jumbo bag of Texas grapefruit, dear, because it's the best price. If I remind her that only she and Ashley will eat grapefruit, Jeanne will tell me to put the bag back and never mind the grapefruit. She craves it, she'll say, but she loves me and wouldn't want to make trouble. I heft the jumbo cartons and bags into the cart without saying a word. It's easier to throw away moldy fruit than to speak up.

If I'm not with Jeanne when she goes shopping, a bagger will load purchases into the trunk of her car while my mother-in-law carefully stands up from the electric cart and positions herself near the driver's seat, facing out. She bends at the waist and falls into the seat, her legs no longer strong enough to lower her body to a sitting position. On the way home, she drives through a fast-food place to purchase a king-size Diet Coke.

She arrives home—sweating and panting, her color leached from the effort of breathing in the heat and humidity—to sit and rest and do a breathing treatment. I put aside whatever I'm doing to make trip after trip from the car to the kitchen, putting away cans and boxes and frozen foods we'll never eat.

She regularly buys canned hams. I have never seen her eat them, but when I helped her clean out her Nebraska pantry before we joined households, I carried twenty-two canned hams to the food bank. Now, in our shared kitchen, I never let the count get that high. Some of what she purchases goes straight into a hidden donation pile. She never misses it, never takes inventory. Her fun is in the buying, not the possessing. She can't stop, I suppose. A friend once told me I was crazy to feel annoyed that my pantry was being filled with food a few times a week. "You should be thankful," my friend said.

But I am not thankful. I want my pantry to myself.

I dream: Jeanne calls for me and when I come to the kitchen she is standing on top of the counter without any clothes on. *She'll fall,* I think, *she has osteoporosis, she's too large for me to lift, how can I get her down?*

She speaks in nonsense syllables. I recognize the words but can't catch the meaning.

My youngest daughter tugs at me from behind and I tell her to run for help, Kayla, run find Daddy, dial 911.

Then Kayla climbs into the bed with me as I pull myself up, up from confusion and into the land of waking.

This dream haunts me because I don't know how it will end.

When our extended family household relocated from Pennsylvania to Texas, we formed a caravan with Jeanne's car and our minivan. Early in the trip I offered to trade off driving her car so she could sit in the passenger's seat with Todd for a couple hundred miles. I thought I would enjoy the solitude. But after only an hour I could no longer stand the cigarette-spoiled perfume smell in her car. Even with the windows open I felt sick to my stomach. By the time we stopped for dinner, my clothes stank. In the foyer of the restaurant Todd bent down for a kiss and then pulled away, repelled. "Your hair smells like cigarettes," he whispered. "Yuck. You smell like my mom."

After dinner I handed Jeanne her car keys, and she seemed happy to drive alone for the rest of the trip, down through summer rain in Virginia, across Tennessee, lush with kudzu, into sunny Arkansas, and on toward Texas. Jeanne drove in her little smoky car just behind our minivan. She held the cigarettes low in case we looked in the rearview mirror.

The first couple of years we lived in Texas, Jeanne drove everywhere—though she avoided the freeways and no longer took major road trips. Now she mostly stays home—close to her oxygen concentrator, her nebulizer, her meds. All the years she drove cross-country alone, the lung disease was her secret. We all thought it was just a smoker's cough, that she was prone to allergies and colds—until we'd lived in Fort Worth two years and Jeanne came down with that Christmas cold she couldn't shake. When her lips went gray and she felt desperate for breath, I took her to the emergency room. The nurse asked about preexisting conditions. Jeanne listed them: arthritis, high blood pressure, atrial fibrillation, COPD. *COPD?* When I got home that night I checked the Internet. Lung disease. Emphysema. How could we think for all those years it was just a cough?

Another dream: She remains clothed, zealously stringing nonsense words together as before. Her dream self watches me intently, the way a dying man watches the living with hungry eyes. It's the way Jeanne looks at me when she's very sick and sorry I have to do so much for her. Full, wide eyes with depth of thankfulness and sorrow. Her words make no sense. Or perhaps they do if I listen with heart and memory for what's underneath each syllable.

There's a poem by William Carlos Williams about rainwater on a red wheelbarrow beside white chickens. *So much depends upon*, the poem begins. The images in this poem draw me back through time to my sixteenth year, when my family relocated from California to Oregon and I saw the world magnified through the poem's glazing of rainwater. All things were connected to all other things. The rain greened the grass and sloshed mud onto the soles of our shoes. Lined up outside the front door were three or four or five pairs of muddy shoes in varying styles and sizes, telling the story of who we were and where we'd been and whether we were home or afield. The wheelbarrow from the poem was there, too, so hard to keep steady with a heavy load of mud-bound sapling roots in planting season. Yellow chicks from the feed store at Easter grew until by summer they had become the poem's white chickens, hoarding eggs in the strangest places. We chopped and plucked all but the one hen my little brother had named Maxwell Smart, who died of old age long after she stopped laying.

✧

"Map of Dallas," Jeanne says, holding it out to me. "You want it?"

"Sure, Mom, thanks." I lay it on the table, knowing I'll never use it, in these days of GPS and OnStar, of Internet mapping programs. Folded maps are a thing of the past, like crew cuts and bobby socks. Let her think it's still useful. I'll slip it into the recycling bin later.

Everything from her glove compartment reeks. The scent of cigarettes penetrates her possessions much as the lung disease grips her life. The smell will fade while the disease grows stronger and steals what independence she still has. Her body now betrays the old secrets. Breath mints don't disguise the wet cough and rough breathing. The electric cart and oxygen tank can't be quickly dropped and trodden under heel. Time has scraped away the layers and exposed what's underneath.

"Don't know why I ever bought this map of Dallas," she says. "Wishful thinking, I guess."

"So what's the plastic knife for, Mom?" I ask, "You gonna ward off a carjacker with it?"

We share a laugh. "Oh, my," Jeanne says. "I like the way your mind works, Lisa. But I do need to keep the knife. I use it when I go on long car trips."

I know who she once was, that she was independent, and strong. She must realize that she won't take any more road trips. Why keep the knife? Why pretend? Even as I feel the pathos of this moment, symbolized by a dumb plastic knife, I understand only in part. She drove across the country, alone, to help someone who needed her. That's why she shops and stocks up. Not for herself—for us.

"I bring crackers and a jar of peanut butter on long trips," Jeanne says. "Then I use the knife to spread peanut butter on crackers. Don't have to waste time stopping in at a restaurant. Done this for years."

"Let's toss the knife, Mom," I say softly. "Get a new one if you—when you go on a trip again."

"Oh, no. Leave it there. I'll need it."

This plastic knife is mystery and symbol to her. Tucked in the glove compartment it is a talisman, evoking the feeling of anticipation, of watching the horizon across long roads of possibility—the independence and the secrets of traveling alone.

"Okay, Mom. Just let me throw it away and replace it with a clean one."

She holds out the yellowed knife, surrendering it to me.

"That'll be fine, dear."

So I get a new knife from the pantry, this one clear plastic, and I place it in her glove box.

Yearning

Birds of a feather flock together
And so will pigs and swine
Rats and mice will have their choice
And so will I have mine

Nursery rhyme

The Tuesday after Labor Day the three older girls go back to school in their plaid uniforms, backpacks stocked with sharpened pencils, pink erasers, and for Laurie in middle school, a compass and protractor. I write a note and place it in seven-year-old Jessica's lunch tote: *I love you—from Mama.* Laurie and Ashley inform me they've grown too old for lunchbox notes.

All through the morning I work on a writing project while sitting in the loft at the top of the stairs. Since school let out in late May I've craved time alone. It is bliss to have a mostly quiet house, to write in broad daylight with only an occasional interruption from three-year-old Kayla, who is content to play in her bedroom. Ideas come fast and my fingers fly across the keys. Ninety-five words per minute with no mistakes. When I'm thinking about what to write next, my hands hover over the keyboard.

Jeanne's slow footsteps scuff down the hall from her suite, and I type my words within her steps—three words for every footfall. When did her stride become a shuffle? I wonder if she can hear me up here in the loft. If I stop typing and duck down on the floor, out of sight, will she think I've taken Kayla and gone to the public library? If only she would go back to her sitting room so I can stretch out the solitude for another thirty minutes, until Kayla gets hungry for lunch.

Jeanne stops at the foot of the stairs. I hear her; I feel her. Silently, she waits. I know she will wait ten, fifteen minutes for me to notice her standing there. What was I about to write? Some added thread, some new tension—but now the thought is gone. I save my file and close my laptop. From the bottom of the stairs, she watches me, her hand resting on the banister.

"Oh, I wondered if you'd had lunch yet," Jeanne says. "I was about to have a bite."

I'd planned to make Kayla a quick sandwich and carry my own lunch upstairs to eat while fact-checking on the Internet. There is so much I could get done before I have to pick up the older girls from school. I hate to lose momentum by stopping for lunch. It feels so good to be focused and productive—to be alone.

"Be down in a sec," I say.

I make sandwiches for Kayla and myself while Jeanne reaches for a bowl from the cupboard and moves soup cans around in the pantry. She selects one. I slice the sandwiches diagonally, put our plates on the table, call for Kayla to wash her hands and come.

Jeanne crimps the soup can with the opener but can't pierce the lid. A lot of things take longer for her to do in recent years, her hands slowed by arthritis, her gait slowed by fear of falling. I hand Kayla a napkin and tell her to start eating, and I step to the island and crank open Jeanne's can of soup. I can't help being irritated with her for moving so very slowly. By the time Jeanne sits down to eat, Kayla will be nearly finished with her lunch. I could have been back upstairs by now, working on my writing project. But I will wait and sit down to eat with Jeanne. She hates eating alone.

While her soup heats in the microwave, I unload clean dishes from the dishwasher. The microwave beeps; Jeanne roots in the drawer for a pot-holder. She takes her bowl from the microwave, stirs the soup, then sets it back in and presses buttons to finish heating. I load the dirty breakfast dishes, add soap. The microwave carousel turns the soup bowl as the timer counts down in increments that seem much slower than seconds. I wipe the counter. It takes me three minutes to unload the dishwasher, thirty seconds to wipe down the counters. If I keep moving, I can get a lot done in the time it takes to pop a bag of microwave popcorn. Or heat a bowl of soup. Even as Jeanne and I sit down to eat together, I'm thinking of getting back to my laptop. She'll want to lie down for a nap after lunch, as she always does, and then I'll have my time alone.

❖

I grew up in Southern California, an oldest child and only daughter. I always had my own room. When I was thirteen we moved to a newly constructed home, and my parents gave me what the blueprint called the "guest room." My tiny attached bathroom had a high window for ventilation. When I stood on tiptoes I could see the neighbor's driveway. Late at night I watched Kerry, the seventeen-year-old next door, making out with her boyfriend. Once I looked out around midnight to see Kerry and her boyfriend climbing onto his motorcycle. The boyfriend pushed his feet against the ground to propel the motorcycle down the driveway—the same way my three-year-old brother, Christopher, pushed his Tyke Bike down our driveway. They coasted the motorcycle down our hilly street about a block before starting the engine and sneaking off into the night.

When I was sixteen, my family moved from California to Oregon, and once again I had my own bedroom with an attached bath. My room was a refuge located deep in the house, at the end of a back hallway. Our 3,000-square-foot rambler on a hilltop outside of town was so huge, Mom joked that we could get lost in it. A parent doing laundry or dishes in the south wing of the house could call and call and the teenager in the bedroom wing would never hear a thing.

In springtime I wandered our twenty-four acres, took long walks down the west hill to stop at the creek and admire pussy willows and cattails. I sang at the top of my lungs from the middle of a field of tall standing hay, because not a soul could hear me. I hope we can move from the suburbs before Laurie turns sixteen, before it's too late for her to wander and think and dream and sing at the top of her lungs because no one is close enough to hear. I long for my girls to know what it is to wander, to explore, to get a little lost and find your way back again.

Like me, Jeanne was an only daughter. When Scott was born, then Jeff, then Todd, Jeanne wished for a baby girl. Her mother-in-law, who had only sons herself, said to Jeanne, "Just wait, dear. Your sons will bring you your daughters." And they did. Three daughters-in-law and six grand-daughters. Mother Harris was right.

Soon after Jeanne and Dewey were married, Dewey went off to serve in Korea and Jeanne lived with her in-laws out in Texas Hill Country between Lockhart and Bastrop. Jeanne and her new mother-in-law grew close; after raising two boys all those years, Mother Harris finally had a daughter. When I married Todd, Jeanne told me how she would treasure that same closeness with me. I resisted. But we have become close, as close as any biological mother and daughter. How did this happen?

Todd's dad died soon after Ashley was born. Todd and I had been married six years, and still I was not close to Jeanne. But there she was alone in Nebraska, with one son in Hawaii and another in Africa. We were in the Middle East. I pictured Jeanne alone in the house in Hastings, with no one to cook for or chat with. How would such an extrovert fare when plunged into the solitary life? I began e-mailing daily, recounting cute toddler stories and cross-cultural confusions, just to keep her company in her lonely first year as a widow. After having established a comfortable emotional distance from Jeanne in the early years of my marriage to Todd, I'm the one who finally pursued and drew close to her, e-mail by e-mail, day after day.

When we returned to the United States two years later, the daily e-mails slipped naturally into daily phone calls. Jeanne got an 800 number so I could call her without paying. If I had it to do over again, would I have called her every day? I can't say. I might have been the more lonesome one at that point, home with three preschoolers and hungry for adult conversation. Phone calls became holiday visits became shopping together for real estate. It's hard to trace our steps back up the slope to see how we got to this point. Much as I want to blame her, she didn't push her way in. I invited her at every step, held her hand and coaxed her all along the way. It seemed right. This is the hardest thing I've done, sharing a household with a woman who is not my choice, not my flesh, not my own mother. It may be hard, but it's only for a season, I tell myself. Except the four seasons begin and end—we may not know precisely when one season is going to roll into the next, but we know the dog days won't last forever. The snow will stop falling and the daffodils will bloom. This season of caregiving stretches on and on with no sign of change, only Jeanne's decline and growing dependency. Is it enough to *do* what I know is right, even though I don't feel it in my heart?

In anticipation of cooler fall weather, I'm changing filters for heating vents throughout the house. As I enter the in-law suite, Jeanne sits at her desk, with her back to me. The desk and window frame her silhouette, backlit by the afternoon sun.

I set up the stepladder and unwrap a fresh filter. Jeanne turns in her swivel chair to watch me.

"Oh, thank you, dear. You do so much for me."

"It'll take just a sec for me to pop this in the vent."

While I unlatch the vent cover and pull the old filter out, Jeanne stands and shuffles toward the bathroom. Her back is crooked, I've noticed in the past year—not really hunched, but one shoulder stands taller than the other.

I pull down the old, dusty filter and drop it carefully at the foot of my stepladder. I push the clean filter into place and clip the vent cover closed. I descend and start to collapse the ladder. Jeanne returns with a duster—she hasn't gone to the bathroom at all. She wanted me to dust the vent cover while I was up there, but she's slow, so slow.

"Oh, you can dust it next time, dear."

"No, Mom. It'll be easy."

I open the stepladder again and climb the two steps to reach up with the duster and swipe the bits of dust and fluff clinging to the vent cover. Jeanne stands at the base of the stepladder, just below me. I work slowly and gently to be sure the bits of fluff and debris are caught in the duster rather than knocked down into her face.

She reaches up to take the duster from me and, as I reach down, time slows as my hand touches hers.

Around the Table

Two, four, six, eight
Being even is just great!

Arithmetic jingle

Our five kitchen chairs are 1970s pieces — but not in that groovy, retro way. These are captain's chairs, low and caramel colored. Comfortable. Over the years, one of the caramel chairs has become wobbly. This doesn't matter for the girls—but if Todd or Jeanne or I sit on it, the chair's legs strain outward. I need to buy wood glue, but I keep forgetting.

Todd and his two brothers grew up with these chairs. Jeanne pulled them out of her basement for us years ago, when we returned from the Middle East. Now seven of us sit around a table meant to comfortably seat six. Todd uses an unmatched chair I picked up at an imports shop, and Kayla sits in an old-fashioned wooden high chair, without a tray, pushed up to the table.

Tonight I'm serving spaghetti, with a choice of shredded mozzarella or parmesan instead of meat sauce for Laurie and Ashley, our young vegetarians. I don't often make spaghetti—just not a dish I enjoy all that much—but the girls love it and dig right in. Jessica sucks up a noodle like a long worm, leaving a dot of sauce on the tip of her nose. Todd and I laugh out loud.

Jeanne comments, "You girls shouldn't slurp your noodles. It's bad manners."

Todd's eyes meet mine.

"Mom," Todd says and shakes his head slightly, trying to signal to her.

"Laurie," Jeanne continues, leaning in and peering down the table. "I thought I told you to eat politely."

It's not that we don't require table manners of our girls. Napkins in laps, eat with utensils, chew with your lips closed, swallow before you speak. But spaghetti is fun—or at least it should be.

"Mom, the way Laurie is eating is just fine," Todd says.

Jeanne lays down her fork and glares at Laurie. Todd and I make conversation, try to act like nothing has happened. Eventually Jeanne begins to eat, but the rest of the family finishes the meal long before she does. I tell the girls they may clear their places, but Todd and I stay at the table.

"May *I* be excused now?" she asks.

"Oh, Mom," I say.

"Here's the thing," Todd begins. "Lisa and I are the parents here, not you. It's hard for us when you correct the girls, because we want them to respect you—but we might have a different take on what's appropriate."

"I thought we were a family," Jeanne says crisply.

"Of course we are," I say. I'm completely perplexed why this isn't making sense to her.

"If we're a family," she says, "I shouldn't have to walk on eggshells. We three adults should be equal partners in parenting these girls."

Todd looks as stunned as I feel. Seriously? She wants to be a threesome?

"Mom, I think we're going to have to agree to disagree on this one," Todd says. "Lisa and I are the girls' parents. You are not."

"Well then, I will refrain from talking to my grandchildren," Jeanne says. She gets up from the table and walks back to her in-law suite.

"Wow," Todd says.

"I hope she doesn't take it out on Laurie," I say.

What we don't realize in this moment is that Jeanne has not always been like this—she hasn't always jumped in to correct the girls. This is a recent development. Perhaps it has to do with her aging, somehow, with her desire to be a vital part of the household, to be needed. She will be tightlipped for days, giving us all the silent treatment until one afternoon when Ashley leaves the front door hanging open and Jeanne calls after her to close it. Ashley will obey her grandmother, and suddenly our household will slide back into tenuous harmony.

The three younger girls don't remember a time before G-Mom lived with us. They don't remember her house in Nebraska, don't remember their G-Dad. Only Laurie remembers what life was like in a true nuclear family. Nowadays Laurie spends her time playing alone in her room and holding her pet guinea pigs; she has begun to avoid entering her grandmother's part of the house. I can't blame her. I suppose wanting time alone is a natural part of entering adolescence, but I can't help feeling like Jeanne is driving Laurie away from our family.

Days later when I call to the girls that dinner's ready, please tell Dad and G-Mom, I notice that the unsteady caramel chair has migrated to my place. Quickly, as the kids are running to wash hands and get to the table for grace, I flip the chair over, its legs in the air, and with a whack of my palm to the side of the chair I knock the loose crosspiece back into its hole. I turn the chair upright and sit down hard. The chair holds, but I know the joint will work loose again in another couple of meals.

"Lisa, I want to buy us a new set of chairs," Jeanne says when we finish grace and start to pass serving dishes. Todd pours milk for the girls while I help Kayla to cut up her meat.

"My legs are pushing the table," Kayla says. "My knees are bumping."

Jessica outgrew this chair when she was a year younger than Kayla is now.

"Mommy, I want to sit in a big girl chair."

"These chairs have had a good life," Jeanne says, "but you should find something you like and let me buy new ones for us."

Jeanne is so generous. I could ask her for anything, and she would gladly purchase it—a new washing machine and dryer last summer, new fridge the year before that, help with the summer A/C bill every year. And now all I can think is, *I don't want new chairs.*

I don't want seven around a table that's made for six. The arrangement is temporary, and eventually the five caramel chairs and the extra from the imports shop will be enough. I keep thinking it will all fix itself, in time, every family problem, the household tension, the shortage of cara-mel chairs.

Long-legged Kayla doesn't know why Mommy is reluctant to go chair shopping; she only knows she's a big girl now and it's not comfortable to have her knees crammed up against the table.

Easy Fix

This little noun
Floating around
Names a person, place, or thing
With a knick-knack, paddy-whack
These are English rules
Isn't language fun and cool?

Shurley Grammar jingle

Kayla pushes the elevator button. When we reach the fifth floor—telemetry wing—we step off the elevator. I feed a dollar into the vending machine and show Kayla which buttons to push. Out slides a cold Diet Coke.

"Careful not to shake the bottle. Give it to G-Mom when we get to her room."

It's November, not quite a year since Jeanne's Christmas cold. I brought her to the emergency room two nights ago because she was coughing and couldn't breathe—and it keeps happening. Last month I brought her candy corn in a mug shaped like a black cat. This hospital stay we've decorated her room with pilgrim figurines and a basket of fall gourds. Looking at these holiday decorations around the hospital room, I can't help remembering the doctor's prediction, and I wonder if Jeanne thinks of it, too. Kayla gives G-Mom the Diet Coke.

"Thanks, sweet pea," Jeanne says. She hands over the TV remote and Kayla starts flipping channels until she finds a children's program. Never mind that it's in Spanish.

Dr. Fletcher arrives on his morning rounds.

He listens to Jeanne's lungs and heart while sitting on the hospital bed beside her. He removes the stethoscope from his ears and hooks it around his neck.

"Good breathing sounds," he says. "The antibiotics are working."

"That must be good stuff they're giving me," she says.

"You were last hospitalized just a month ago, Mrs. Harris. And you have such frequent exacerbations. Are you still smoking?"

Jeanne looks Dr. Fletcher straight in the eyes. "No. I quit smoking a long time ago."

He looks to me, and I back her up. "She's not smoking," I say.

"Well then, something else is wrong. We'll start by having you see the endocrinologist. Maybe the cardiologist, too. I'll extend the order for your home health nurse another six weeks. You should not be getting pneumonia this often, Mrs. Harris. We'll figure out what this is."

History is taught chronologically at the classical school our girls attend, starting with Ancient Egypt in second grade, Greece and Rome in third, the Middle Ages in fourth, and on through to sixth grade for the Civil War to present. In seventh grade the cycle begins again, with deeper studies the second time through. Students take Latin from third grade through high school.

Todd is headmaster at this school, which is located thirty minutes from our home. He uses the commute time to listen to audiobooks with the girls—he makes the car trips fun. I drive the same freeway into town to take Jeanne for medical appointments.

One by one, the possible causes for Jeanne's frequent pulmonary infections are ruled out. Finally Debbie, Dr. Fletcher's nurse, takes yet another blood sample. "Dark red and healthy," she says as the vial fills. "You must eat a lot of meat."

Jeanne is a rancher's granddaughter. She grew up in the Texas Panhandle eating meat and potatoes with creamed something on the side. She married a man who took his meat so seriously he got a PhD and went to work for the USDA breeding swine, "the other white meat." Every Easter

Jeanne insists on giving me money for an expensive spiral-cut ham, never noticing that she and Todd are the only ones who eat from it. "If you don't serve meat it isn't a meal, it's a snack," Jeanne says.

I stand in front of the open case in the meat department and glance over the hunks of flesh. I have no idea what differentiates one cut from another. I pick up a package and examine the beef labeled "beef round thin cut steak"—but how would I cook it? In a fry pan? Crockpot? I hate using the broiler—I *won't* use the broiler. So gross to clean. I turn the package over for cooking instructions, but there aren't any. I don't even own steak knives, and I could go a year without eating a potato. Oh yes, my mother-in-law eats a lot of meat. And I am the one who cooks it for her.

✥

Lab reports come back with news that Jeanne is completely missing one immune factor: she has something called selective IgA deficiency. The IgA class of immunoglobulins protects the body's mucous surfaces from infection—including mouth, throat, and lungs. Not a good immune deficiency to have alongside lung disease, but it explains the frequent infections.

I take her to see an immunologist, who tells us Jeanne should receive monthly infusions to replace the blood factors her own body doesn't produce, thereby boosting her immune system. The procedure is expensive—more than five thousand dollars per infusion—but Medicare will cover the cost. Jeanne will go to the same center where cancer patients receive chemotherapy. Nurses there will settle Jeanne in a comfortable chair and find a vein. The IV bag will drip the blood product into Jeanne's system, and in four or five hours she'll come home. The immunologist explains that she may feel very tired immediately after the infusion, but most patients feel a surge of energy on the second day. It may take a few months, however, before Jeanne will really hit her stride and see sustained improvement.

"Easy fix," the immunologist says. "You'll have energy, and you'll feel better than you have in years."

"It's good to try new things," Jeanne says with a grin. "Let's do it."

✥

Todd and the girls love to watch science fiction shows. They watched one recently in which the protagonist and his assistant travel back to London during World War II air raids. I kept hearing a tinny child's voice from the TV room saying, "Are you my mummy?"

When I asked the girls what the episode was about, they answered, "Nanogenes." Nano*what*? This is why I don't watch much science fiction myself. Nanogenes, the girls explained, are some kind of biological medical therapy that can heal wounds and bond with a patient's DNA to make up what the body lacks, sometimes even bringing a patient back from death.

If Jeanne were a time traveler, maybe nanogenes could heal her IgA deficiency.

The first infusion takes five hours. Jeanne dozes in the car on the drive home afterward, doesn't want to eat anything. She climbs into bed and sleeps through until the next morning, when she wakes exhausted. A month later she is just as fatigued after the second infusion, and two days after the infusion, when she should be feeling that surge of energy, she has coughing and shortness of breath. An x-ray at Dr. Fletcher's office shows a new nodule, a spot on her lung.

"We'll check it again in three months," Dr. Fletcher says. "Probably just something that didn't clear up from your last pneumonia."

One Saturday I open a fresh length of oxygen tubing and replace the one Jeanne has been using for a few weeks. Ashley swings a length of discarded tubing back and forth like a jump rope. She and Jessica sing:

> Cinderella dressed in white
> Went upstairs to pick a fight
> When her dad saw she was cranky
> He said, "You must have a spanky!"

The girls burst into giggles. I hold out my hand to collect the tubing. It makes a decent jump rope, but I don't want them to think they can play with Jeanne's medical supplies.

"We're trying to make up a rhyme about Cinderella for every color," Jessa tells me.

"Nice," I say. I chant the words to "Fudge, Fudge, Call the judge," then I sing "The Lady with the Alligator Purse." The lyrics are horrid—discarding a newborn baby in an elevator, a baby drinking bathtub water, eating soap, and worse. Did I listen to what I sang as a child? My girls don't hear the words; they are enchanted by meter and sound, not meaning.

At dinner I raise the topic of children's rhymes with awful lyrics.

"There's 'London Bridge,' too," says Laurie. "That's about a bunch of people dying when a bridge falls on them. And 'Rock a Bye, Baby.'"

"Wow," I say. "I really never listen to the words, do I?"

"You know about 'Ring Around the Rosy,' don't you?" Laurie asks. She studied the black plague last year in fourth grade.

"Yes," I say. "That one I know. Ashes, ashes, all fall down."

✧

Three months later we return to Dr. Fletcher's office for the follow-up x-ray. Jeanne wears a blouse with snaps rather than buttons.

"I'm a modern woman," Jeanne says to the nurse, deadpan.

"Well, good for you, Mrs. Harris," Debbie says. "Now let's just have you step into the x-ray booth and unbutton your shirt."

In one movement Jeanne grasps her blouse and yanks it open, revealing that she is braless. Debbie snorts and laughs. "Hey, we are not supposed to have this much fun in here," she says. The x-ray machine beeps and clicks.

"Mrs. Harris, did you know you're my favorite patient?"

Jeanne smiles as she snaps her blouse closed. "Let's just keep this our little secret," she says. "But now you know how liberated I really am."

Dr. Fletcher checks Jeanne's lung sounds and asks her how she's doing.

"You tell me," Jeanne says. "You just looked at my x-ray, didn't you?"

"Mrs. Harris, I see a mass," he says.

This is it. This is how it begins. I imagine her in a hospital bed, gaunt and weak and struggling to breathe.

He wants to do a PET scan, which, he explains, is the last noninvasive tool before cutting a patient open or sticking a big hollow needle in between the ribs and into the lung to bring out a core sample for biopsy. The PET shows malignancy with 95 percent accuracy. To figure out what type, doctors still have to cut or poke a hollow needle down deep to extract tissue.

Cancer. I've always assumed Jeanne would one day get lung cancer. Now we're here. Jeanne's face shows no expression. I wonder what she's feeling right now. Dread?

"Is a PET scan painful?" she asks.

"No, not at all. You do have to fast for twenty-four hours beforehand."

Jeanne will be injected with a radioactive glucose substance that will be allowed to circulate in her body for about an hour before the scan. The high-tech PET imaging will register areas of her body that absorb a lot of radio-glucose. The fast-growing cells suck up more glucose and show as "hot spots" on the scan.

A diagnosis is not final until cells have been examined under a microscope, most likely via a fine-needle aspiration. If the PET scan doesn't have any hot spots, then there's no need for further testing. If the PET scan shows hot spots, then we move on to the biopsy to see what we're dealing with.

"I'll have Debbie schedule the appointment for you," Dr. Fletcher says.

Jeanne nods and says, "Okay, then."

❋

When Laurie had the hiccups recently, I told her to swallow a spoonful of peanut butter. Todd said she should hold her breath. Jeanne said to drink a cup of water while holding her nose.

"Mainly," I said, "keep your mouth closed and your hiccups will be silent."

"I could scare you," Todd offered.

"Stand on your head," Ashley suggested.

"Maybe nanogenes," Jessica said.

Kayla simply watched the drama with big eyes. Nothing worked, and Laurie went to her room alone. By the time she returned for supper, the hiccups were gone.

Ask anyone how to cure the hiccups. "Works every time," you'll hear with each suggestion. Compile a list and when you get hiccups, try the home remedies on your list, one after another. If nothing works, don't fret. The hiccups will go away in an hour or a day. That's your easy fix for hiccups. Wait them out.

I wish it could be as easy for Jeanne.

❖

"I'm hungry for Tex-Mex," Jeanne says on the way home from Dr. Fletcher's office.

I drop her off at the entrance to Abuelo's and drive around to find a parking spot. She waits at the door, then takes my hand and we walk in together. Jeanne orders pork tamales and I ask for tortilla soup with avocados and extra sour cream. The server brings fresh chips and salsa. We order a side of guacamole.

I resolve that when Jeanne asks me to go someplace, to take her out for lunch or shopping, or just for a drive, I will say yes and not make excuses, not think about my writing or myself. She may have cancer. I need to always say yes.

The food arrives, and we eat.

"Mother used to get us tamales from a little Mexican lady in Amarillo," Jeanne says. She takes a bite and chews, swallows, sips her Diet Coke.

She tells me about growing up in Amarillo, about her grandfather who ran cattle and her father who traveled to Mexico City on business, bringing home gifts and treats.

"Ah, tamales," Jeanne says. "Definitely one of the better things in life."

Comfort Food

Intery, mintery, cutery, corn
Apple seed and apple thorn

Nursery rhyme

I woo Jeanne's appetite with her favorite foods. Grits, banana pudding, Miracle Whip and bologna loaf on white bread. French dressing over cottage cheese. Sausage gravy over biscuits: pallid sauce so thick with grease that the leftovers will congeal, gray and lumpy. Tomorrow I will reheat them to mash over her toast.

When she first moved in with us, years ago, I made things my way: stir fry, one-pot dishes, beans and rice. She ate only after fishing out the veggies. If I used tofu, she asked, "What's this stuff?" and pushed it aside. And yet she bragged, "Lisa is such a good cook!" Years passed and I learned to reserve a handful of raw veggies for her plate; she loved vegetables, as it ended up—just not cooked my way.

Back when I was Todd's girlfriend, Jeanne invited her minister and his wife, among others, to a dinner party. She cut the greens quickly with scissors and tossed the salad in a large trash bag. She made the entire meal a day ahead, so when the guests arrived we all were relaxed and ready, and all she had to do was reheat. I remember chicken in a cream sauce that night, a salad with honeyed almonds and red onions. I remember the smell of garlic cheese bread rising as the minister said grace. I remember bringing the savory bread to my mouth and crunching in to find that instead of garlic butter under the melted cheese she had spread Miracle Whip, warm and cloying. After a long wash of ice water to get the hunk down, I poked at the rest of my meal.

Once I had a ring on my finger, I volunteered to make the cheese bread whenever she cooked Italian. And when I had the Harris name firmly attached by vows to my own, I also picked the red onions out of my salad and laid them on the side of my plate.

In recipes calling for milk I now substitute heavy cream. Jeanne has lost seven pounds in two weeks and we're not sure why, except the doctor says the mass in her lungs—three months ago the size of the doctor's retractable pen clicker—is now the size of both his hands fisted one over the other.

What the tests will show, what the future will be, I do not know. What I do know is this: break the sausage apart as it fries in the pan; sprinkle in flour to absorb the grease; add heavy cream and stir until the sauce is thick and no lumps remain. Spoon the mixture over biscuits or toast and grind fresh pepper on top. When I bring it to her, the plate will be warm through. She will take and eat.

Epistaxis

Did you ever think as the hearse goes by
That you might be the next to die?

Skipping rhyme

"*Is G–Mom going to die?*" Jessica asks.

"No, honey. People don't die of nosebleeds."

"Yes, they do," says Ashley. "Like Attila the Hun. Seriously."

"Attila the Hun?" I say. "Died from a nosebleed?"

"He choked on his own blood," Ashley says. "Because he was drunk."

"Ew, that's just gross," says Jessica.

I'm driving a little over the speed limit, taking the girls into Fort Worth to meet Todd, who will take them the rest of the way to school. Of course the one morning we have an emergency, he's already all the way across town at an early-morning school board meeting.

I merge into the exit lane and glance at my watch. Fifteen minutes already. Another fifteen to get back home. Todd is here at the meeting place just ahead of me, and as the girls clamber out of the minivan I roll down my window.

"Is Mom okay?" Todd asks.

"I don't know," I say. "There's a lot of blood. I shouldn't have left her alone, but we were already so late. I hate this."

"Oh, sweetie," Todd says. "I'll bring the girls home after school. Promise you'll call me from the hospital."

❖

I had been on my way out the door to take the girls to school when I realized Jeanne hadn't gotten up for her morning breathing treatment. I told the girls to get in the car and went to check on her. Jeanne's pillow and gown were soiled, and she'd screwed tissues into a wad and stuffed them up her nose. The bloodline seeped almost to the edge of the tissue.

I thought of the Coumadin—stroke-preventing blood thinner—Jeanne takes each evening and the warnings that come with it, and my legs felt shaky.

"I woke up when I felt the flow," Jeanne said, "but I've made such a mess for you."

Bloody mucus stretched from her right nostril as she pulled out a soiled tissue and replaced it with a clean one. I watched the bright blood soak through, soiling the fresh tissue within a minute. Jeanne breathed from her mouth, still wearing her oxygen tubing with its bloody cannula providing an oxygen flow over the tissues that plugged her nostrils.

"Okay, Mom, let's take off the oxygen."

"I want to call Dr. Rubin when his office opens."

Dr. Rubin is Jeanne's general practitioner, and his office is a half mile from our home. But he doesn't open till ten, and it was not quite seven-thirty.

"When did the nosebleed start?"

"Four o'clock this morning."

"And it's been bleeding the whole time?"

She nodded. Jeanne hates the emergency room, hates going to the hospital. As a result, she waits too long before confessing her symptoms to me and by the time we finally do go to the emergency room she needs to be admitted.

"Lisa, why don't you check the Internet?"

I swung open her computer cabinet and keyed "nosebleed when to see doctor" into the search engine. I clicked on the first result.

"If a nosebleed lasts longer than twenty minutes, seek medical aid," I read aloud.

"All right," she said quietly.

"I have to take the girls to school," I said. "When I come back, we'll go to the ER."

❖

I've never dealt with a serious nosebleed. Once, as a small girl, I remember lying on my back while my mother sat on the couch beside me and stroked my hair. I remember a cold wet rag under my nose and my mother's hand on my head. I don't remember any blood.

I arrive back home relieved to find Jeanne conscious, though discouraged.

"I thought it would stop by now," she says.

I help her take off the bloody gown and get dressed. We bring a box of tissues and an old, stained hand towel out to the car. Jeanne sits in the passenger's seat, head bowed with her right hand cupped on the side of her face so the neighbors won't see. I run back into the house to quickly pack an overnight bag. I hold the bag low and slip it into the rear of the van before getting into the driver's seat and backing out of the driveway.

"What about the PET scan?" Jeanne asks as we pull out onto the freeway.

The scan is scheduled first thing tomorrow morning, with a required twenty-four-hour fast beforehand.

"I've started fasting," Jeanne says.

"Let's just see what they say, Mom."

Could lung cancer cause a crazy nosebleed? We drive in silence to the emergency room.

There are as many home remedies for nosebleeds as there are for the hiccups. Inhale drops of fresh lemon juice into each nostril several times daily. Pour cold water over the head or place ice under the nose. Grind equal parts dried lotus flower and hard candy; take one teaspoon of lotus-candy powder with hot milk morning and evening for one week. A few drops of onion juice mixed with mint leaves may be drawn into the nose to stop bleeding. Take sugared milk with a banana: after one week, the nosebleed will be cured. Hold the flat side of a cold butter knife to the nape of the neck, drop keys down the back of the shirt, or otherwise run a metallic object along the patient's spine.

The first thing the emergency room doctor does is put a clamp on

Jeanne's nose—nothing more than a fancy sterile clothespin. The clip works a little better than the wadded-up tissue, effectively preventing the blood from dripping down Jeanne's face. It drips down the back of her throat instead. Jeanne coughs and spits bright blood into an emesis basin. When the nurse enters the room to draw blood, Jeanne jokes that we should fit the vial to her nostril and fill 'er up. The nurse smiles vaguely and draws blood in the traditional manner.

The doctor explains that the blood labs are simply to rule out a clotting problem caused by the Coumadin. He removes the clothespin and shines a light up Jeanne's nose, holding it open with a delicate speculum that doesn't look much different from the needle-nosed pliers in my toolbox at home. He can see the source of bleeding in one nostril, but not the other. The doctor removes the speculum and has Jeanne gently blow, then he inserts rolls of sodden gauze.

"These are soaked in an astringent," the doctor says, "a small percentage of cocaine. The solution should shrink the blood vessels and stop the bleeding." He'll return in ten minutes to remove the gauze, he tells us, so we can go home.

Blood soaks through the saturated cotton and drips onto Jeanne's clothing. I step out to call for a nurse, but the halls are empty. Where is the call button? I yank open drawer after drawer full of medical supplies until I find gauze pads. I hand her a stack and go to find help. Treatment after treatment fails, morning flows into afternoon, and Jeanne is still bleeding.

❖

My first memory is of a hospital. I was three years old, and my mother had just given birth—a new baby brother. Visiting children were not allowed upstairs, so I had to stay in the lobby. I stood on a chair and stepped over the armrest to the chair beside it—to the next and the next, without ever touching the floor. An elevator door opened and my father called, "Lisa!" He stood smiling beside Mom, who was in a wheelchair—but no baby. I ran to them.

"Where's the baby?" I cried.

"Look here, Lisa," Mom said gently, and she showed me the baby lying alongside her slim hips on the wide seat of the wheelchair. "This is Erik," she said. "Your new brother."

This baby boy would grow to be a stubborn, wiry kid who built elaborate forts in the backyard and occasionally stepped on rusty nails—a kid who rode his bike with no hands and caught air doing bike jumps, Evel Knievel style. At eleven, Erik watched the older boys in the neighborhood build a quarter-pipe skateboard ramp, off of which he would one day fly, cutting open his chin and breaking his jaw in both joints.

The doorbell rang and Mom opened the door, expecting a Jehovah's Witness or the Avon Lady, but there stood Erik, bleeding down the front of his shirt. She pulled him inside and hollered for me to bring clean rags. Mom knew she had to apply pressure to the wound before he lost too much blood, but when she pressed the rag to his chin he screamed and fought back. She continued to press firmly: first step, stop the bleeding. When she removed the rag to evaluate the wound, she saw bits of sidewalk grit embedded in her boy's flesh. The chin clearly needed sutures, so she drove Erik to the emergency room, leaving me home with our four-year-old brother, Christopher. Kerry, the teenager from next door, came over at Mom's request to keep me company so I didn't worry too much.

I wasn't worried. Erik was always getting hurt. Kerry and I stood around the kitchen for a little while with not much to talk about. Her T-shirt said in rounded iron-on letters, *Manitoba is Number One.*

"Isn't Manitoba in Canada?" I said, trying to make conversation. "Did you ski there or something?"

"No," Kerry said. "Manitoba is the name of my boyfriend's band. They're outa sight."

I felt a little embarrassed to hear Kerry say "outa sight," but I tried to act cool.

"So, what do you want to do?" I asked.

"We could make some prank calls," she said.

I didn't think we should, but Kerry knew pranks that weren't mean, just funny. *Is your refrigerator running?* She used the downstairs phone and I used the extension in my parents' bedroom. Christopher played with toys in his room.

Mom brought Erik home with twelve stitches in his chin and instructions to return in three days to have the jaw wired shut, once Erik was past the danger of vomiting from a severe concussion. Technicians had taken x-rays, moving Erik's head and jaw into this position and that. The initial images were unclear, so they called him back into x-ray and tried again. Twelve x-rays later, not one film was clear. Finally the pediatrician sent Erik out of the hospital and down the street to the oral surgeon's office, where a panoramic dental x-ray was taken painlessly and an appointment scheduled for the wiring.

"I tried and tried to call," Mom said when they arrived back home. "Something's wrong with the phone line—busy signal every time." I didn't confess about the prank calls, but I was ashamed of myself. Here my brother had broken his jaw in two places and I hadn't worried about him for even a moment.

In another time and place, before local hospitals and emergency rooms, Mom might have stopped the bleeding, cleaned out the wound, even sutured it herself with a needle and thread. The broken jaw might have been diagnosed, a century ago, by symptoms alone, but without the magic of an x-ray no one would have known the jaw was broken at the joints. A jaw fracture can affect facial nerves, leading to numbness. One hundred years ago, Erik's jaw might have mended wrong, and he might have grown up with a facial deformation and permanent pain, unable to speak or eat like everyone else.

The medical staff had equipment and training and could properly irrigate, disinfect, and suture Erik's wound. They had strong painkillers, access to a panoramic x-ray machine, antibiotics to prevent infection, a vaccine for tetanus, and a way to wire the boy's teeth shut so his jaw would properly heal.

✧

When I take Jeanne to the hospital emergency room, I expect safety, assistance, professionals who know what I don't about medical treatment, who have access to medications and equipment I don't have at home. Come in with a nosebleed that won't quit and what do they do? If the clothespin doesn't work, shove a wad of gauze up her nose and wait to see what happens next.

I've been in several hospital emergency rooms through the course of my parenting—usually false alarms when the blood was far worse than the wound—once a severe croup episode that required Ashley to be hospitalized. Every ER I've been in feels like the catacombs. Follow the blue line on the floor to get to the exit. Red line to the bathroom. Remember the cubicle number, because once you've taken a couple of turns it all looks the same.

I want medicine to be like it is on the sci-fi shows. The doctor waves a sensor over the patient and a diagnosis pops up. Shots are given without needles; bones are mended instantly. "Take care, that was a bad break," the starship doctor may say. "It will be tender for a few hours." For all the gruesome aliens and fierce battle scenes, the medical bay is bloodless in the imagined future. That's what I want—I want medicine to have the answers; I want painless treatments but would settle for treatments that work. I want the doctor to be God.

From within the fluorescent halls of the ER, with all its beeping and monitors and stripes painted on the floor, I feel I'm in a cave. Things are still primitive. Even if you make it to the emergency room, even if the doctors find a treatment that works this time, someday you will surely die.

❖

"It's just a nosebleed," Jeanne says. "I want to go home."

The doctor's manner changes abruptly. "I can see you aren't happy about this, Mrs. Harris," he says. "I'm sorry. We could just take you straight up to surgery right now."

"I don't want surgery," Jeanne says in a small voice.

When the nurse comes, Jeanne tries again. "I don't want to have my nose packed," she says. "A friend had it done and said it was the worst pain she'd experienced."

"Well," the nurse says, "it's better than bleeding to death."

Emergency room protocol for the treatment of epistaxis starts with the least invasive treatment—the fancy clothespin—and moves up the ladder of procedures from direct pressure and vasoconstrictors to cauterization to packing the nose with gauze or a nasal tampon. If the gauze or tampon fails, a sophisticated two-part epistaxis balloon is inserted deep in the nares and then inflated. The rear extension of the balloon fills the posterior nasal opening deep between the eyes, while the front of the balloon applies pressure from the bridge of the nose to the opening, the anterior. The procedure is painful and often requires sedation. There is a likelihood of infection and airway compromise. Severe epistaxis may require intubation.

Cautery controls Jeanne's bleeding in one nostril, but the other side appears to be bleeding from the posterior, deeper than the doctor's flashlight can illuminate. He inserts the very long deflated roll of balloon deep into her nose: in and in and deeper in. She gags. Slowly he inflates the balloon. Jeanne's face grows pale. The opposite nostril begins to bleed again, and the doctor carefully inserts a second long balloon so far into Jeanne's bleeding nostril I have to avert my eyes.

"Painful," Jeanne whispers as he inflates the second balloon. "Oh, it hurts."

"We'll admit you overnight," the doctor says. "We need to start vitamin K infusions to reverse the Coumadin."

Within minutes a nurse arrives with morphine.

❂

Jeanne will later say that it wasn't better than dying at all.

"I'm going to die one of these days anyway," she'll tell me. "Worse if a stroke leaves me damaged, or if my breathing gets horrible—I'm so scared of that."

How long does she have? Death is inevitable for all of us, but urgently inevitable for an elderly patient with a chronic or terminal illness.

"Would it be so bad to bleed to death?" Jeanne wants to know.

We would never withhold treatment for a simple nosebleed. Balloons inflated in her nose, morphine for pain, the breathing troubles she will have for weeks afterward, and all of it in the middle of wondering if Jeanne has cancer, knowing her health is failing and if it isn't cancer it will be something else.

The patient is not offered a choice. We treat. Jeanne is shamed into doing what she doesn't want to do in a myriad of small treatments that add up to lots of pain and frustration and helplessness. She is forced to endure pain in order to live in continuing pain. No one asks what Jeanne wants. If you don't want to live, you wouldn't come to the ER. I can't advocate for her—they'll think I'm homicidal. I also couldn't have let her stay home and bleed, could I, even if that's what she wanted?

It's too awful to think about.

Todd joins me in the ER in the early evening, once he's settled the girls at home with our friend Kathleen there to watch them. Jeanne is finally moved to a room upstairs, nearly twelve hours after our arrival at the ER. I'm shocked to see that she's not in the telemetry wing like all the other times she's been hospitalized.

"She uses oxygen at night," I tell the nurse. Someone brings oxygen tubing and rigs up a mask to go over Jeanne's mouth. "She has an immune deficiency," I say. "Shouldn't she be on antibiotics?" The nurses soothe me like I'm a hysterical child. The doctor has not ordered antibiotics.

"She may have cancer," I say quietly. "We had a PET scan scheduled. Could cancer cause this excessive bleeding?" The nurse shrugs.

Blood crusts the fine netting that covers the packing balloons, which extend a half-inch from her nose. A long string hangs from each one, and I resist the morbid impulse to grab and pull. I stare at the balloons, sure they're slipping out, ever so slowly. Fresh blood oozes at the edges. The nurse assures me that everything's fine.

We say good night to Jeanne and return home to our girls. Ashley asks Todd to help her study for a Latin test. As I put on my nightgown I hear her high, strong voice chanting conjugations: *Moneo, mones, monet. Monemus, monetis, monent.* I warn, you warn, he/she/it warns. We warn, y'all warn, they warn.

Waiting

Tommy's tears and Mary's fears
Will make them old before their years

Nursery rhyme

Jeanne looks awful when she is discharged from the hospital the following day and comes home to rest in her own bed. Bloody blobs hang out of each nostril, but Kayla and Jessica climb up on the bed and kiss Jeanne's cheeks. They snuggle close and ask about the dried blood and the strings hanging down from each nostril and whether it hurts; these little girls aren't afraid of how G-Mom looks. Jeanne says she feels constantly short of breath. Her face is pale. She won't eat.

My biggest fear is that Jeanne will get another respiratory infection before she has the packing out of her nostrils. She is coughing a little, coughing up blood she swallowed during the twelve-hour nosebleed. Her coughing has been much calmer than usual, maybe because of the morphine and now the Darvocet—I've read that narcotics can help to ease shortness of breath and coughing. Whatever the reason, Jeanne is not struggling to breathe, and I'm thankful.

She will wear the balloons for three days, and then we'll see the ENT to have them deflated and removed. I have a call in to reschedule the PET scan.

I'm helping Jeanne set up her nebulizer for a breathing treatment when Kayla asks me to read to her. I tell her I'll come in a minute, just let me finish helping G-Mom. By the time I've taken care of Jeanne, Kayla has started playing with her sisters and doesn't want me anymore.

❀

"Do you think my mom is dying?"

Todd and I are sitting upstairs in the loft, and we can hear Jeanne downstairs in her sitting room, coughing a little. She can't hear our conversation over the blare of her television set.

"I don't think there's any way for me to know," I answer. "But I do feel she's leaving us, little by little." Her breathing is worse than it has ever been before, even when she's had pneumonia. I hear rasping and wheezing. She looks like every breath hurts. But Jeanne has color in her face—she's not blue around the nose and lips like I've seen in the past.

❁

Jeanne develops a sinus headache, even with the painkillers, and I immediately suspect infection. We see the ENT a day early to have the balloons removed. Sure enough, he writes Jeanne a prescription for antibiotics.

We stop on the way home for takeout, and Jeanne eats a sandwich and fries along with her Diet Coke. "Never again," Jeanne says. "If I have another nosebleed, then that's the way I'll die." The nosebleed is behind us, but the PET scan is rescheduled for next week. Now we wait.

Culture Shock

Needles and pins, needles and pins
When a man marries his trouble begins

Nursery rhyme

When Todd and I were first dating, his mother met us after a conference in Kansas to drive us four and a half hours to her home in Nebraska.

We left Wichita early, stopping for breakfast at Hardee's after we'd driven an hour or so. I'd never even heard of Hardee's. Country ham, sausage biscuits, eggs and cheese and fatty breakfast meats. Not even a plain biscuit option. My fast-food breakfast culture in the Pacific Northwest always included a basic choice of fruit and a bagel or bran muffin. I scanned the overhead menu more and more frantically as Todd, and then his mother, easily made their choices. They both ordered Diet Coke—Diet Coke for breakfast?—and the cashier looked to me.

"I'm not so hungry. Umm, I guess I'll just have the orange juice," I said.

Todd and his mom tucked into their biscuity, meaty breakfasts with lots of reminiscing about eating at Hardee's when they used to live in Indiana. Todd grew up in West Lafayette, where his dad worked for the USDA on the campus of Purdue University. Todd's parents were both Texans, but his father's career had pulled them north, and all three of the Harris brothers were raised in the Midwest.

With a refill of Diet Coke to fuel the drive ahead—Diet Coke for breakfast!—we got in the car and Jeanne headed us toward Nebraska. I sat in back with Todd, like a kid. His mother's short, dark hair, flecked with gray, was cut close over the ears. She wore wide sunglasses and kept her eyes on the road, talking to us without glancing in the mirror for eye contact. Jeanne stood five-foot-seven in those days, five inches taller than I was. She seemed so large. Like royalty reeking of cigarette smoke. Jeanne didn't need a map to cross that flat grid. Just head north on I-81 all the way, she said. Two hundred miles of sameness, Todd and his mom cracking open Diet Cherry Cokes from her cooler and driving, driving, driving across the endless loop of flat fields. I'd never driven for long without coming to a mountain range or the Pacific Ocean. I'd learned to drive on roads that twisted up and down mountainsides. In my landscape, you could never really see where you were going—always mystery ahead over the next curve, around the next bend. In this landscape, flat fields stretched all the way to the horizon. Seemed to me there was *more* need for a map on this terrain. Each mile looked the same. Out beyond the freeway, farm roads ran along property lines and crossed at intervals, unmarked. In Kansas, in Nebraska, how do you know when to stay straight and when to turn right? Miss a turn in this geography, and you'll drive fifty miles out of your way before you realize something's not right.

When Jeanne stopped for lunch, she paid—even for me. Should I protest? Push cash across the table or grab the ticket and calculate my portion? At twenty-seven I had been on my own for years. On road trips with friends I always pitched in for gas, split the tab at lunch. Jeanne stopped for gas and handed a twenty over the backseat to Todd. "Let's get us some snacks," she said. What was I to do? I went with the flow, feeling increasingly like a child and not a woman in her midtwenties.

❖

When we arrived in Nebraska, Jeanne wheeled her own suitcase into the house. Todd grabbed his duffel and I lifted my carry-on from the trunk. The entry from the garage opened through the laundry room into a dark kitchen, embellished everywhere with owls. Needlepoint owls filled the walls, owl figurines lined the windowsill, and a ticking owl's belly showed the time while its round shifting eyes marked the seconds.

"Give Lisa the middle room," she said to Todd, and he led me down the spiral staircase to the daylight basement. Upstairs, the telephone rang.

Todd showed me my room and where to find the bathroom at the end of the hall.

"That's Dad," she called down the stairs. "He's coming home. Dinner in forty-five minutes."

We came back up the circular stairs and I asked, "What can I do to help?"

"I've got dinner ready to go. Made it before I went to Kansas for you all. I just put it in the oven. Par-mEE-jun chicken," she said. My fingers itched for a dictionary.

"Let's go for a walk," Todd said, opening the front door.

Once outside, I turned to him and asked, "What did she say we're having for dinner?"

He pronounced *Parmesan* the way I'd always heard it pronounced.

"Just checking," I said.

Their house was situated on several landscaped acres about five miles out of Hastings. Standing on the front porch, we looked out across to a winter cornfield. Todd took my hand and we walked down the gravel road. The neighbors kept pygmy goats, a donkey, and two ostriches. We squinted into the sunset. Nebraska. I let go of Todd's hand and turned slowly in a circle.

"So flat," I said. "Like we're in the middle of a huge pancake. The road just goes till it disappears."

"There's a lake if you keep going far enough," Todd said. "And my dad's work is basically way down this same road. A couple of turns and you're there."

"What does he do, again?"

"Works for the USDA. Breeds meatier pigs or something."

I wanted Todd's parents to like me. Todd was moving to Oregon soon, our plans still unspoken above a whisper. In another month we would be engaged—married by the end of summer. These were my future in-laws. Grandparents to my future children. We came in from our walk, and I hurried to wash my hands and help Jeanne set the table.

Todd's dad came in and laid his briefcase and jacket on the counter. As Dewey gave Todd an awkward side hug, Jeanne whisked the jacket and briefcase off to another room. I didn't know Dewey well, and I wanted to make a good impression. So when he invited me to come out to the Meat Animal Research Center the next afternoon to see where he worked, I quickly accepted even though Todd had declined. Jeanne offered to drive me, but I insisted that I was comfortable driving myself. Maybe this short trip would make me feel like an adult again.

"I'll write you directions," Dewey said. "Getting there is easy as pie."

❖

The next morning, a piece of paper lay on the kitchen table with my name on it. Dewey had drawn a map to his workplace. I wished he'd included verbal directions with the schematic, but it looked straightforward enough. A hashmarked train track intersected what must be the gravel road in front of the house, and that's where I was to make a left turn just after crossing US 281. Right turn at US 6 and there's no missing the Meat Animal Research Center. The scale of the map made it look a few blocks away.

Jeanne gave me her keys. "Sure you don't need me to drive you, dear?"

"Oh, I'll be fine. I have the map."

As the car tires crunched down the gravel road, I imagined myself parking at the research center, walking in the door, and confidently striding up to the desk to ask for Dr. Harris. The secretaries would steal glances at me and whisper admiringly that I was the son's girlfriend, visiting from the West Coast.

The train tracks came too soon, and the roads weren't marked. I looked at Dewey's map again. Yes, definitely train tracks. And I'd crossed them, followed the correct turns. According to the map, I should have passed the research center by now. To my right, farmland. To my left, the same. Billowing dust announced an approaching pickup truck. As the driver passed me, he raised his hand lightly off the steering wheel and gave a nod.

I turned the car around—five point turn between dirt-road ditches in a boat of a car. I found the right road, a familiar silo, and drove slowly back to the house, tears burning down my cheeks.

Jeanne drove me to the research center, turning at a second set of railroad tracks, miles farther than the first. That thirty-minute drive fore-shadowed so much of our future together as mother- and daughter-in-law. I couldn't have known then. Calculate the time Jeanne and I have spent alone in a car together over the years, multiply by miles per hour, and the total would reach all the way from my home in Oregon, backward across the Oregon Trail and the flat Midwest, cross the Platte where Jeanne loved to sit in her parked car and watch the Sandhill cranes, and reach all the way to the eastern seaboard, to Philadelphia where Jeanne would move in with Todd and me just after our tenth anniversary. And then 1,500 more miles southwest, back to Jeanne's home state of Texas, where we would move as an extended family just in time for Todd and me to celebrate being married for twelve years.

What We Don't Know

Mother, mother, I feel sick
Send for the doctor quick, quick, quick
Doctor, doctor, shall I die?
Yes, my dear, and so shall I
How many carriages shall I have?
One! Two! Three! Four!

Skipping rhyme

Jeanne uses saline spray each morning and evening to keep her nasal passages moisturized. All these weeks since the nosebleed, and she's still not breathing comfortably. I don't know whether to expect her to fully recover or if this is her new baseline.

I research types of lung cancer—some kill quickly while others linger. Jeanne and I don't talk about it directly, but she says to me one day, "You know how I've always said no chemotherapy? Well, if something like chemo could help me breathe better I might want to try it."

Today is finally the day of Jeanne's rescheduled PET scan. I load the oxygen tank into the car in the space behind her seat and snake the tubing around her seat belt.

I drive around the perimeter of the building, but there are no handicapped spots. Before the nosebleed, I would have dropped her off at the door and then gone to park, but she is now too weak to walk any distance without extreme shortness of breath.

I see red taillights and wait for a car to back out so I can claim the newly vacated spot, parking to the far left, my driver's-side tires just inside the white line. This allows enough room on Jeanne's side of the car for me to bring the wheelchair right up beside the passenger's door.

"I don't need to wear the oxygen inside," she says. "Just bring it." She removes the tubing from her face and hands it to me. I push the wheelchair and tow the oxygen tank behind us.

"Cancer and Blood Disorders," Jeanne reads aloud as we pass the sign in front of the entrance. "Lisa, this can't be the right place."

"Mom, all the signs say that."

Does she not realize? When Dr. Fletcher said, "Something that hasn't cleared up on the x-ray," and "large spot on your lung," and "probably need to biopsy," I saw the word *cancer* twisting and knotting itself between his words. Instead of looking at the doctor's face, I watched Jeanne. All she said was, "Okay then. We'll make the appointment."

❀

I was six years old when my maternal grandfather's heart gave out. He had dozed off in a living room chair before Sunday dinner, and by the time he was called for the meal, Grandpa was already gone. We were living far away in Southern California, and my mother wasn't able to attend her father's funeral, held three days later in Montana.

The night of my grandfather's death, I dreamed that I sat cross-legged in the grass with a circle of other children and with Jesus, who wore white robes and had chestnut hair and eyes, just like the pictures in Sunday school. Instead of teaching a lesson or passing around hunks of fish and bread, Jesus reached out for me and I climbed into his lap. Tears streamed down his face.

My paternal grandfather, a Swedish immigrant, was diagnosed with colon cancer when I was in college. When Grandpa Emil was receiving hospice care at home, Mom and Dad quickly planned a trip to see him one last time. Erik and Christopher went with them to say good-bye, but I refused to go with them. I reasoned that I wanted to remember Grandpa strong and steady—not weak and thin and drugged for pain.

A week later I rode with my parents and brothers up to Seattle for the funeral. When the body was raised up in the casket for viewing, I slipped out the back into the foyer, with my brothers and younger cousins close behind.

I last saw both grandmothers at my wedding in Oregon. Months later

I heard that my paternal grandmother was no longer lucid and the family up in Washington State was providing care for her at home, and a few years after that I got word my other grandmother had passed away. By the time either of them grew frail, I was living too far away to come say good-bye or to help with their care.

✿

At the Cancer and Blood Disorders clinic Jeanne and I sit in the waiting room with the tank of oxygen between us, closed tightly.

To our left, an older couple sits reading. The nurse opens the door, calls a name, and the woman closes her paperback and stands. The husband watches over his newspaper but remains seated.

"How are you today?" the nurse asks.

"Oh, I'm fine, just fine," the woman answers. Her forearms are bruised below her short-sleeved shirt, just like Jeanne's. The husband smiles at me and settles back to read his paper.

Jeanne huffs and breathes deeply, first through her nose and then with open mouth. The oxygen canister sits between us, the tubing gathered neatly like a lasso around the arm of her wheelchair.

✿

My childhood home in Southern California had a tall willow tree in the front yard. In spring, the willow grew tiny, hard bullets that softened and stretched over the weeks to release seeds on paper wings. Past the willow was the neighbor's driveway, a driveway Mom crossed a few times a day to visit her friend Marilyn.

Marilyn had multiple sclerosis so advanced she was already in a wheel-chair by the time her kids were teenagers. She spoke in what sounded to me like slushy vowels and groans, but my mother understood every word. From watching Mom and Marilyn's friendship I learned that someone in a wheelchair, someone with spastic hands and legs, is a whole person and can be a friend. I learned not to feel awkward around a person with a dis-ability. I fantasized that I, too, understood Marilyn's speech—but I never really did.

I would have my chance for friendship long in the future, when a young man on campus, a journalism major, looked my way. Troy was known for his weekly column in the student paper. I watched him ride his three-wheel bike across campus quarter after quarter, and I felt a brief thrill when I saw him—not a crush, but a brush with fame. One day Troy held a door open for me on campus, and I introduced myself. We became good friends.

Troy had cerebral palsy. His articulation was wide and imprecise, but I understood him just as Mom had understood Marilyn. When Troy laughed, all loose and joyful, it didn't matter whether my midterms had gone well or I'd gotten the part I wanted in the spring play.

"Let's get together," I'd say to Troy.

"Meet me in my office," Troy would answer, his "office" being the donut shop across from campus.

One day I cooked lunch for Troy at my place, but when he asked for a straw to drink his water without spilling, I felt ashamed, because I hadn't thought to get straws. All those times we'd eaten together at the donut shop and I hadn't made note of the fact that he always drank through a straw. I wasn't Troy's caregiver, but I was his friend. Shouldn't friends notice the little things?

Mom, Marilyn, Troy. The fact that I lived far from my grandparents when they were old and dying—none of this explains why I was willing to share a home with my mother-in-law, who was neither disabled nor ill nor elderly when we signed that mortgage together. But my history might just explain why I'm not afraid to touch frailty, not afraid of wheelchairs. It might explain why I didn't want Jeanne to be alone after Dewey died, why I wanted her to grow old with us and not under someone else's care far away.

The nurse holds the door open and calls Jeanne's name. I maneuver the wheelchair and oxygen tank through the door.

"You're doing so well with that," the nurse says to me. "I'll just open the doors for you."

She escorts us to a small room with a huge overstuffed recliner in it. I lock the wheelchair and take Jeanne's purse from her lap so she can stand and pivot to sit in the recliner. The chair is so big her feet don't touch the floor.

"I need to ask you a few questions," the nurse says. The radiologist rubs Jeanne's arm with a cotton swab and he pulls a rubber tourniquet tight above her elbow before tapping for a vein.

"Now," the nurse says, "have you had any operations? List the surgery and when you had it."

"My hysterectomy," Jeanne says. The radiologist inserts his needle. "Oh, my. I can't think. Todd was three."

"That would have been around nineteen seventy," I say.

"Gallstones in the midsixties," Jeanne adds. "And the benign tumor I had removed from my back . . . when was that?"

It was the month Dewey died. "Nineteen ninety-seven," I say.

"Yes, that was it," Jeanne nods.

"Next question," the nurse says. "Have you had cancer before?"

Jeanne doesn't answer for a moment. Then, in a quiet voice, "I've never had cancer."

The radiologist asks Jeanne not to talk anymore, to lean back and rest; he'll return in an hour to give the glucose time to spread through her system. When he and the nurse leave the room, I open the valve on the oxygen canister and hand Jeanne the nasal cannula. She places it over her face without a comment. There is no second chair, so I sit in the wheelchair and read while Jeanne dozes.

No wonder people think I'm her daughter. It's not just that I push her wheelchair—I know Jeanne's family history, can remember details better than Todd does. I've learned what her face looks like when she needs more oxygen; I see that her nose is dripping and hand her a tissue before she feels it herself. Todd is willing, but he doesn't see what needs to be done, doesn't help without being asked. He does notice how very much I do for his mom, and he thanks me regularly. But somehow I don't think he sees all the small ways his mom needs help—like me with Troy's straws, years ago.

We've been in Texas five years, and Jeanne has been frail for almost two. When we came, Todd was headmaster of a small school. In addition to running the school, he taught a Latin class, he spent time with students, with their parents, with his faculty. But the student body has doubled and Todd's job has become mostly administrative—deskwork rather than the team-building, mentoring, face-to-face job it was in the early years. Todd is ready to move on. He talks about finding a position directly under a head of school, so he can still be an administrator but not topmost in the chain of command. Does such a thing exist?

"There's a job opening in Wenatchee," Todd said recently. "Could you remind me again why we can't move with Mom?"

We have this conversation often. Even though I long for my girls to have space to wander, to sing loudly where no one can hear them, I push down my desire and repeat the litany of reasons why we can't move yet. Jeanne is on oxygen full time now. She can't drive. How would we get her across the country? She can't fly. She can't go up or down stairs. She has all these specialists in Fort Worth—just fifteen or twenty minutes away. I don't want to live in the suburbs again if we can help it, but if we don't live near a big city, how far would we have to travel to get Jeanne the medical care she needs? The last time Jeanne got an infusion, there was an older man there whose wife drives him an hour and a half for his chemo treatments. They bring sack lunches and they make a day of it. I point out to Todd that if Jeanne had gotten sick when we lived in Pennsylvania, we could have been driving an hour into Philly for her medical care. Yes, I want to get on with our lives, I want Todd to be happy in his job, I want our girls to have open spaces—but not at such a great cost to Jeanne and me.

"Forget Wenatchee," Todd said. "I know you're right. I just wish there could be a way."

"It's a season," I said.

An indeterminate season with signs of change we don't know how to read.

An hour after the radioactive glucose injection, I help Jeanne from the huge recliner back into her wheelchair, and the radiology tech pushes her into the room with the PET scanner. He helps Jeanne up onto what looks like a long plastic tongue extending from the wide-open mouth of the scanner. He swaddles Jeanne's arms in a blanket and gently lifts the oxygen tank so that it rests on the platform below her legs.

"You'll have to wait in the lounge," he tells me. "It will only take about thirty minutes." On my way out, I pass through the control room, behind glass like the mixboard in a sound studio. Two more techs—or radiologists, or whoever they are—sit on rolling stools in front of the monitors that will soon show where in Jeanne's body the glucose gathers. They'll see the hot spots. By the time I come back in thirty minutes, they will know whether she has cancer and they will know if it has spread.

While waiting, I scope out the best way to exit the building with a wheelchair and I locate a soft drink machine and buy Jeanne a cold Diet Coke.

The radiology tech finds me waiting near the Coke machine. Jeanne is already seated in the wheelchair. I pull the tank and push the wheelchair, while the radiologist opens doors. "Most people try pushing the tank," he says. "Your way works much better."

We exit the clinic, and I push her wheelchair back past the sign that reads Cancer and Blood Disorders. Neither of us says a word.

Results

If all the world were apple pie
And all the sea were ink
And all the trees were bread and cheese
What should we have for drink?

Nursery rhyme

"*I should call Harry and Cathy,*" Jeanne says. We're watching her favorite morning news and talk show as I drink coffee and she sips her first Diet Coke. "I haven't talked to them in weeks."

"Good time to call," I say. "It's early, so they're probably still home."

"I'll wait until after we've seen Dr. Fletcher," Jeanne says. "I want to be able to say either I have cancer or I don't have cancer."

Now I know she understands what news we may receive today.

"I just don't want to be in pain," Jeanne says. "I know you'll respect my wishes, Lisa. But what will Dr. Fletcher think of me? I don't want treatment. He won't be on the same page."

"Mom, who cares if he's on the same page? It's your life, not his. Anyway, we don't know what he'll say."

An hour and a half later we're waiting for Dr. Fletcher. I feel nervous and shaky—but not weepy. This will be much easier to get through if the emotions don't hit. I need to drive us home afterward.

Dr. Fletcher enters. "How are you today, Mrs. Harris?"

"That's what I'm here to find out," Jeanne says.

Dr. Fletcher explains that the growth in Jeanne's lung absorbed more of the glucose solution than the surrounding tissue, but not much more.

On the scale of cancer probability, it's low. Possible, but not obviously so. Maybe early stage—very early. There's a chance it's not cancer at all.

"So from here we can do a biopsy," he explains. "Because of your lungs we'd need to do it in the hospital, and you'll be sore afterward."

"What if she doesn't do a biopsy?" I ask.

"Then we would simply do a CT scan in a few months," Dr. Fletcher said. "And another a few months after that. Watchful waiting."

Jeanne's voice is a little too loud, almost harsh. "Will you still be my doctor even if I don't get the biopsy?"

Dr. Fletcher chuckles. "I'll still be your doctor, Mrs. Harris."

"And if I have cancer but I don't want treatment—will you still be my doctor?"

"Mrs. Harris," he says, "you can't get rid of me that easily. Of course I'll still be your doctor. This is exactly what I would do in your situation."

The clock above Jeanne, I notice, is the same color and shape as one of her steroid inhalers. It bears the name of the inhaler's pharmaceutical company.

I came here braced for cancer, whether a fast-growing small-cell cancer or a more typical, slower-growing large-cell lung cancer. I'm ready to put aside my life for six months or a year, to be Jeanne's best friend, to keep my life on hold while she lives out hers. But it's not late-stage cancer—probably not cancer at all. Whether she has a diagnosis or not, she needs my help more and more. How many more years will she be alive and failing?

We drive home in silence. Jeanne suggests we celebrate by getting Chinese takeout for dinner—her treat. When we get back to the house, Jeanne sits on the side of her bed and asks me to pull off her slacks and shoes so she can take a nap.

"I may not have cancer," Jeanne says, "but I sure feel puny."

Tornado

Old Grimes is dead, that good old man
We ne'er shall see him more
He used to wear a long brown coat
All buttoned down before

Nursery rhyme

"We'll just have to cross our fingers," the vet says after checking Tornado. "Put the heating pad under her cage when you get home and say a prayer."

Laurie nods soberly and kisses Tornado right where the guinea pig's brown fur swirls in a permanent bedhead. The vet gives Tornado a steroid shot and sends us home with extra vitamin C and not much hope.

Laurie had awoken me about two this morning. "Tornado's not acting right," Laurie said. "She's scaring me." The guinea pig didn't seem sick so much as off in the head, dashing around her cage and clunking into the sides like a drunk.

In the dim light from the hallway, I moved the guinea pig's cage, a large storage bin without a lid, out of Laurie's room and into our open loft. It was the night before the last day of school, and Laurie needed her sleep.

"Mom, what if she dies? We have to do something to help her."

"I don't know, Laurie. We can try and see the vet first thing."

"I don't want to miss the living history museum at school, but I can't leave Tornado."

"We'll see about Tornado and I'll take you in late."

I tucked Laurie in, my tall twelve-year-old girl, and as I turned to leave the room I saw her James Madison costume laid out on the desk: knickers, a shirt with ruffled collar, and cardboard buckles painted gold and glued onto her black shoes.

In the light of morning, it's clear that Tornado's water bottle is untouched, even though it has been days since it was last filled.

✵

When we get home from the veterinary clinic, Laurie settles Tornado in with the heating pad, fresh water, and food. The guinea pig seems perkier already and takes a drink from her water bottle. Maybe the steroid shot did the trick. I check on the other guinea pig. Sarah nibbles at a stem of hay. Dear old Sarah. She's the old lady guinea pig, the one who made the move with us from Pennsylvania to Texas years ago. Lately Sarah's skin has grown crusty in spots, and it's clear she's not grooming herself. Excrement sticks to her hind quarters and her claws. For a year or two now she's had a tumor growing from her ear. When she was young, Sarah was such a pretty guinea pig—but beautiful Sarah was a biter. It is only in Sarah's old age that Laurie can finally hold her without being nipped. Laurie tried many times to teach the two guinea pigs to get along, so that they could live together in the same bin. But Sarah was too aggressive. Eventually, Laurie quit trying.

While Laurie changes into her James Madison costume, I go down to Jeanne's room.

"Hey, Mom. The guinea pig seems better now. The vet gave her a shot and vitamins."

"Oh, that's good news. How is our Laurie?"

"She's encouraged. We're heading to school soon. You feeling okay?"

"I didn't cough as much last night. Still, I'm feeling awful tired."

I tell Jeanne the sandwich I've made for her lunch is on a covered plate in the fridge.

During the thirty-minute drive to school, Laurie practices her James Madison monologue. She falls silent for a few minutes, then says, "Mom, I was ready for Sarah to die, but not Tornado."

Sarah is fat, lazy, and old. Her tumor has a crusty black fold at the end, almost like a foul belly button.

"I always thought Sarah would die first," Laurie says.

When we arrive at the classroom, Sacagewea sits frozen next to Dolley Madison. Laurie takes her place beside a stiff Cortez with a Spanish beard penciled onto his chin. Four-foot-eleven George Washington comes to life and gives his monologue. "I died in 1799 and was buried at my beloved Mount Vernon." James Madison rolls her eyes at me. When her turn comes, the closing line is "I retired at Montpelier, my estate in Virginia."

"Please remember to take your kids' backpacks home with you," Todd says after presenting the final awards. Classmates hug and high five while parents thank teachers for a good year before gathering offspring and backpacks. Outside the auditorium, heavy clouds to the southwest darken the sky. We live southeast of the school. "We can beat the storm," I say to the girls. "Get in the car. Now."

We just have time to pull in the recycling bins and the lawn furniture before the storm hits. The girls are giddy because school is out, and the sky is as dark as twilight at 4:00 in the afternoon. My cell phone chirps Mendelssohn, and I dig in my purse. Todd should be on his way home by now, probably calling to say he's gotten caught in the storm.

"Hey, Todd. Are the roads okay?"

"Not too bad. Did you check on Tornado yet?"

I'd forgotten about the guinea pig. The house is so dark from the storm that we can just see Tornado's outline—she's lying on her side near the water bottle.

"Oh, Laurie. Let me get the light."

I shift the pedestal lamp so we can see Tornado.

"She's breathing!" Jessica announces with relief.

"But she's dying," Laurie says. "Guinea pigs never go on their sides like this."

Laurie kneels down and reaches to touch Tornado. The guinea pig jerks like a cat dreaming of chasing a mouse. She takes quick, shallow breaths, stops breathing altogether at one point, and then starts up again.

By 4:30 I think each breath has got to be the last. Surely this pig won't suffer all the way through another night until morning.

An hour later, with a towel under her armpit where the side of the bin is making her sore, Laurie still holds her hand over Tornado's body. "Do you think she's in pain, Mom?"

"I think she's unconscious, Laurie. I don't think she's feeling any of this, but I don't know."

"I wish she could die quicker. Does this happen with people?"

I tell her about G-Dad's death, about Carolyn's. I tell Laurie how proud I am that she's more grown up and selfless with her pet's death than I was with my own grandfather's when I was twenty and refused to see him because I was afraid it would make me too sad.

Finally at 5:35, Tornado sneezes and bares her teeth, then sneezes again and does not draw in breath.

Laurie weeps in my arms, taller than I am, but still my little girl.

I make boxed mac and cheese—one of Laurie's favorite easy dinners—and afterward we find a shoebox in the garage. Laurie lines the shoebox with soft fabric and tissues while the rain pours. She puts on some latex gloves the home health nurse has left behind, and Laurie holds Tornado's body like a grieving mother might hold a stillborn child. Todd and the girls put on rain slickers and go out to bury Tornado in the side yard while Jeanne and I watch through the window.

"Sweet girls," Jeanne says. "It's so hard when a pet dies."

Recipe

There were once two cats of Kilkenny
Each thought there was one cat too many
So they fought and they fit
And they scratched and they bit
Till, excepting their nails
And the tips of their tails
Instead of two cats, there weren't any

Nursery rhyme

"Did you take my cake recipe?" Jeanne asks.

"Cake recipe?"

"The one with the oatmeal and chocolate chips."

"I didn't touch your recipe box, Mom."

Her eyes narrow. "Well, I can't find it."

I would never go looking for one of Jeanne's recipes.

She speaks again. "And I don't know why you think I need a babysitter."

She means Kathleen, the family friend who will look in on Jeanne while we're on vacation next week. I'm changing my strategy this year—she was so offended when I called Harry and Cathy to come. I thought this would feel okay to her. Just Kathleen dropping by twice a day, morning and evening.

"Why do I need Kathleen?" Jeanne asks.

Kathleen will come because I can't relax on vacation thinking of Jeanne gasping for breath when the oxygen tubing pulls off and she doesn't have the strength to reattach it—or she gets another nosebleed and can't drive herself up the freeway to the ER and won't call for help. I've coached Kathleen what questions to ask and what signs to look for—too many wadded up tissues might mean a respiratory infection that could go to pneumonia. If Jeanne is spaced-out and forgetful, if her lips look pale or blue, then her oxygen level has dropped too far. Someone has to watch for these things. But Jeanne hates to think she needs help.

"What will Kathleen do when she comes? Or is that a secret, too?"

I read that a side effect of steroids can be anger, paranoia. All those prednisone tapers for the lung infections, month after month. The daily doses to keep her lungs as clear as possible. When the dose is increased, Jeanne has nightmares. She declares that the neighbors intentionally point their back porch light to shine in her bedroom window at night. Now she accuses me of hiding a recipe card or making secret plans with Kathleen. I change the subject.

"I'll do all your laundry before we leave, Mom."

"I can wash my own clothes."

Except that she can't bend over to pull clothes out of the dryer. I've done her laundry for years now. I would be irresponsible to leave her alone for a week. No one to open her soup can. Bring in the paper and mail. Close a window on the computer so she can find her e-mail again. Peel the tab off the new milk jug. She doesn't mind asking me to do these things, but she won't let anyone else step in and help.

I hear her now in the kitchen, sighing "Hoh, boy," under her breath. I wish I could call her bluff, tell Kathleen not to come—but I don't have the guts. It would be like leaving a toddler home alone with a gas stove turned on.

Jeanne goes into her sitting room. The TV is off.

I come into the room and sit beside her. She says nothing.

Much of the time I'm the only one who is absolutely honest with Jeanne. She loves me for this when she doesn't hate me for it. I don't know how to make her see how frail she really is, how dependent on me. Maybe there's another way to shoot straight.

"Mom, this vacation—does it bother you that we're going and you're not?"

"No, Lisa, it's not that. It's just that . . ."

She holds her mouth open but doesn't complete the sentence. She closes her mouth. Opens again. Closes.

After a while she clicks on the television set.

Jeanne finds the missing recipe folded behind some others in her file and gathers her ingredients.

"Will you be home for a while, Lisa? I'll need you to lift the KitchenAid up onto the counter for me," she says.

"Sure, Mom. I'll do that for you."

As Jeanne cracks the eggs and measures the oil, she tells me this cake recipe came out of a newspaper in Indiana, years ago, when the boys were small. So moist. It's the oatmeal that makes it that way.

Jeanne used to write the recipe out on extra cards whenever she brought the cake to a potluck, because people would always ask for it. She lost the recipe once before, then recopied it from Aunt Cathy.

"I lose recipes all the time," Jeanne says with a chuckle.

I lift the mixing bowl and hold it at an angle above the cake pan while she spoons out batter. I place the cake pans in the oven, while Jeanne rinses the mixer attachment and loads it in the dishwasher.

I listen for the oven timer, because Jeanne has lost her hearing in the upper range. I move the rounds from the oven to cooling racks for Jeanne to frost.

I will carry the cake to the table after dinner tonight, and then it will be Jeanne's cake. Hers to slice and serve.

A few weeks later, when we get back from vacation, the girls come scrambling into the sitting room.

"G-Mom, look at these cool rocks we found at the river!"

"We picked wild onions and ate them every day!"

"Mommy found a baby scorpion under the sheets!"

Jeanne looks happy, surrounded by her granddaughters. She laughs, reminds them to speak one at a time so she can hear every last detail.

"Look, G-Mom, we brought you a present!" Jessica hands her grandmother the small gift bag, and Jeanne reaches in and pulls out a carved wooden hummingbird.

When the girls disperse and Jeanne and I are alone together, she confesses that after we left, she started coughing up dark sputum tinged with blood and she didn't tell Kathleen. Jeanne called Dr. Fletcher and he said to come in right away or else go to the emergency room. Jeanne said all right and got off the phone. Ten minutes later she redialed and begged him to call in a prescription for antibiotics. Said she was all alone, couldn't drive the freeway, that her daughter-in-law wouldn't be back for several days. She didn't mention Kathleen.

Jeanne drove herself to the pharmacy to pick up the prescription. She had blood in her sputum for two more days and took her antibiotics in secret.

I'm stunned. She should have told Kathleen, should have had a chest x-ray, had her oxygen levels checked. But Jeanne didn't ask for help. I suppose she proved that she could take care of herself. I open, then close my mouth, trying to respond. I have nothing to say.

Cataract Surgery

Four and twenty tailors
Went to kill a snail
The best man among them
Durst not touch her tail
She put out her horns
Like a little kyloe cow
Run, tailors, run, or
She'll kill you all e'en now

Nursery rhyme

It is late September, now nearly two years since Jeanne's Christmas cold. I've been putting drops in her right eye twice a day for several days in preparation for the outpatient surgery. Jeanne has a small, round dot of a sticker above her right eyebrow. The waiting room is full of people, mostly elderly, with stickers above their right eyes. No one else seems to find this amusing.

A thin man in his sixties comes out of the surgery area led by a nurse about his age. He walks like a drunk.

"There now, sit here. We've called your daughter. She'll be right over to take you home."

The man leans to one side in the waiting room chair and dozes.

One eye at a time, they told us. The left eye two weeks after the right. The doctor does right eyes for the first two hours of the morning, and then left. Fewer things go wrong, the nurse said.

A frail woman in a wheelchair smiles at the receptionist, who asks the woman's year of birth.

"Oh, that would be 1919," the woman says sweetly.

"Did you bring your medications?"

The woman smiles up at the middle-aged man standing beside her, "Did I take medicine today, dear?"

The son says something about the nursing home handling the meds and he isn't sure what she takes. The woman smiles vacantly and shifts slightly in her wheelchair. I wonder how her life will improve. Why put her through a surgery?

The nurse calls Jeanne's name.

It never crossed my mind that Jeanne might have cataracts.

In June our car was in the shop, and I rode with Jeanne to go out to lunch together one day. She didn't look behind her before backing out of the driveway. She drifted into the wrong lane. She drove way too slow, even got honked at once. She missed a stop sign at a four-way stop. *It's time*, I thought. *We have to tell her to stop driving*. But we didn't say a thing.

Jeanne must have assumed for some time that she had cataracts. She mentioned her vision problems to me in July and started calling around to find a good doctor. We had to wait until the girls were back in school before starting the process. Last week, the pre-op and eye drops. Today the surgery. Tomorrow an early-morning check on the eye and then across town to the hospital for a CT scan. It has been four months, nearly five, since Jeanne decided to "watch and wait" rather than have a biopsy. She didn't want the CT scan in August, because Jeff was visiting, and then Scott and Michelle. If the CT showed something bad, she didn't want to know—didn't want to ruin our family time. We go back to Dr. Fletcher's office next week for the follow-up. And back to this office for a follow-up on the right eye later that same day, then again the week after that for eye drops to begin the process on the left. I'll drive Jeanne to the hospital for her infusion and to Dr. Rubin for the monthly blood draw to make sure her blood is neither too thick nor too thin, so he can make the necessary adjustments to her Coumadin dosage. Jeanne will wake on the Saturday morning after the CT scan to tell me, "I'm coughing up gunk with blood in it," and we will be at the emergency room all day. Kayla's fifth birthday. One thing will lead to another and even though Jeanne's eyesight will be sharp and clear for the remaining year of her life, she will not drive again.

Even without knowing that Jeanne won't live much more than a year, I wonder, why bother with the cataract surgery? The potential risks are small, but she has to open her eye and let a surgeon at it. I'm not sure I would do it myself.

A nurse invites me back to meet Jeanne in the recovery room. She is wheeled in, looking dazed.

"You're still in Neverland, aren't you?" the nurse says to Jeanne.

"Not a bad place to be at all," Jeanne says.

The surgery went well, I'm told. And I suddenly realize what a good thing this is and how respectful of life. Jeanne's body is damaged and failing in so many ways, but her vision has been restored. And we will learn next week that her CT scan shows no major changes, no new concerns. For a couple of weeks it will feel like Jeanne's resurrected vision is a sign of improving health and hope for a brighter future.

Falling

Out goes the rat
Out goes the cat
Out goes the lady
With the big, green hat

Skipping rhyme

"Wake up," Todd whispers. It's about 10:00 p.m. on a Saturday night in early November.

"Mom fell and she's bleeding. I don't know how to bandage it." I follow him down to Jeanne's bathroom. She sits in the wheelchair by the sink, groping for a package of Band-Aids in the low cupboard. The light in the bathroom is bright.

"Here, Mom, let me see where it's bleeding," I say, feeling my heart beat fast in my neck and even my wrists. This is the second time she's fallen this week. The first time was last Sunday morning when she was home alone. She lay on the floor a long time before she managed to crawl to the toilet and somehow pull herself up on the commode. She can't remember just how it happened. "I got all tangled up," she says.

Jeanne pulls her robe up to expose her injured leg. A large purple bruise has formed over her right knee, extending down her leg, which is scraped in several places and has an outright gash about four inches below the knee.

"Did you fall against something sharp, Mom?"

"Is it cut? I just fell on the carpet in my TV room."

"Mom, do you feel like you broke anything?"

"No, nothing broken I'm sure. Oh, darling, I'm so sorry."

"This will need more than a Band-Aid," I say. From the first-aid kit I take antibacterial ointment, gauze, paper tape. She cringes when the gauze touches her wound. I can't apply pressure—it hurts her too much. On closer inspection I see that the wound is not a gash so much as a wide area of exposed flesh, almost like a burn. Not spurting, but oozing blood. I don't like blood.

"We'll have to go for stitches tomorrow, Mom."

We both know what a wreck the emergency room is late at night. If the bleeding is controlled it will be fine to wait. I wrap extra gauze around and around her leg.

Todd had heard a noise from downstairs as he worked on his computer in the loft, but he hadn't thought it was more than a knocked-over TV tray or a dropped book. Ten minutes later, when he went downstairs to be sure the doors were locked before coming to bed, he found his mom lying on the floor with bruised and bloody legs.

He tried to lift her—she told him to stop. It hurt, how he gripped her. Todd retrieved the wheelchair from the car, and somehow he got her into it and wheeled her into the bathroom. He didn't know how to stop the bleeding or what to do about the carpet stains. Jeanne said he should wake me.

Tomorrow the doctor will tell Jeanne her wound can't be sutured, that there's not enough skin to stitch. In a month he will say it's her poor circulation that makes for slow healing. He'll recommend physical therapy and a cane or walker to keep from falling. In two months he will send in home health nurses and try a new regimen of wound care to facilitate healing. In five months the wound will finally heal enough we can stop bandaging it. By that time she will have given up on physical therapy. She'll use a walker or wheelchair all the time and will be housebound. This wound will get better, but there will be other bandages, and more wounds that don't heal.

But tonight the fact that she fell is new and shocking. The lung disease and oxygen tanks and even the occasional use of the wheelchair when she's out of breath have become familiar accoutrements, but I honestly never thought her lungs would hold out long enough for her to grow frail and start falling. It feels so heavy. We help her to bed and say good night. Jeanne looks up at us and thanks us and again tells us she is sorry. We all know that what happened tonight is a big deal. She fell last week—one fall. Fluke. But tonight's fall begins a pattern. No longer, "she fell," but, "she's been falling."

Autumn Sage

Mary, Mary, quite contrary
How does your garden grow?

Nursery rhyme

The first time it happened was in October. And then again—twice—in November. What better season for falling? The leaves lose their grasp and come floating down, brittle as an old woman's hipbone.

❖

After Jeanne fell for the second time, I bought her a cobalt blue walker with hand brakes, shiny as a new bicycle, but two days later when we left for an appointment with Dr. Rubin, she abandoned the walker inside our front door and reached for me. I took her hand as she lurched down the porch step, lost her balance, then steadied herself against me. My thoughts immediately raced to *don't fall, please don't fall.* At Rubin's office I took Jeanne's hand as we walked into the waiting room and then down the hall to an exam room. I understood, without asking, why the walker had to remain at home. Jeanne was not yet ready to admit she needed an old-lady contraption, shiny blue or not.

"One of my medications must be off," Jeanne told Dr. Rubin. "I just can't figure out why I keep falling."

"We're all getting older," he said. "Do you think you blacked out? Did you feel dizzy before you fell?"

"Oh, no. Nothing like that. My feet just got tangled up."

"Well, let's go over your medications and draw some blood for labs. Definitely use a walker. Silver sulfadiazine ointment on the leg wounds and moist-heat soaks three times a day to increase blood flow and promote healing." We filled the prescription for the special ointment on the way home.

I picked up her lab results the following day, and Chris, Dr. Rubin's nurse, sat with me in the waiting room for a few minutes, chatting. The report showed Jeanne's complete blood count and her thyroid hormone levels as normal.

"It's the steroids," Chris said. "They destroy the protective fatty layer under the skin and make it fragile. That's why it tears so easily and takes forever to heal."

"But that doesn't explain the falling, does it?" I asked.

"Oh, it's just so hard to get old," Chris said.

Fall used to be my favorite season, for all the usual crisp and colorful reasons. A month ago I drove Ashley home from gymnastics class the week after Daylight Saving Time ended, and instead of making our way home through the golden light of late afternoon, all around us was twilight gray. Leaves swirled from the trees and I wanted to weep, because I knew the few that clung to the branches would soon be gone. *I used to love the autumn*, I thought. *What's wrong with me?*

Every morning, while I'm pouring milk on cereal and packing lunches and brushing hair to get the girls out the door with Todd by 7:15, Jeanne pushes her walker down the hall from her bedroom to the TV room, where she sits in her favorite wingback chair and twists open two tubes of liquid steroids. She squeezes the medications into the bowl of her nebulizer and turns up the volume on the TV so she can hear it over the machine's hum.

Once the girls are off to school, I pour myself a cup of coffee and join her. Jeanne smiles at me through the fog of vaporized medication. As long as the nebulizer is running, we do not talk. She needs to breathe every bit of the medicine deep into her lungs.

When the nebulizer's reservoir is empty, Jeanne turns the machine off.

I set my coffee aside and kneel down next to her footstool to peel back the bandage on her leg. She winces as I pull up the gauze pad.

The open wound looks mushy, with a layer of yellowy white over the exposed flesh. It reminds me of chicken fat. The home health nurses use terms like *exudate, metabolic waste, slough*. Every time I remove the bandage I cringe and taste bile. At the kitchen sink I drag a towel through steaming water and wring it out like a washermaid.

"Oh, that feels good," Jeanne says as I place the soaking towel directly on the wound. I cover it with a layer of plastic sheeting and lay the heating pad on top. I set the timer for twenty minutes and leave her to the rest of the morning news. Cloud cover today, the weatherman says. Calm early this morning then breezy and cool, with highs in the midfifties.

❖

After talking with Chris the other day, I came home and looked up "prednisone, side effects" on the Internet. This drug, among the many Jeanne takes, creates a host of problems: cataracts, osteoporosis, thin skin. Prednisone also causes muscle weakness that in turn may lead to falling. The steroid decreases bone density, making the tendency to fall even more alarming. Daily doses puff up her feet and legs with fluid that also pools around her heart and lungs, resulting in even more difficulty breathing. So Dr. Rubin prescribes a diuretic, which makes Jeanne lightheaded and likely to fall again. Along with the diuretic he tells her to take potassium, since frequent urination leaches important minerals and may throw her electrolytes out of balance.

There is no way to reverse the prednisone's damage. We keep adding more treatments and more medications for each side effect, as if it's an independent ailment. I guess we should have read the tissue-thin scroll of fine print that came with the pills that very first time. But what would we have done, even if we'd read the list? She was so short of breath. Prednisone helped.

Each time we come home from the doctor's office with a new prescription in hand, Jeanne is hopeful. She feels as though something's getting fixed, as though a problem has been solved. But in a month or two, the new medication will need its own companion med to treat some new symptom. Still, there is no question that these medications have extended her life. Despite signing an advance directive years ago, she has gradually been put on various forms of life support—oxygen, heart medications, plus steroids in powder, liquid, tablet, and aerosol form. Prednisone has made her veins so fine and delicate that nurses can't draw blood without collapsing a vein. Each failed probe of the needle leaves a dark bruise on her arm.

Time to talk to your immunologist about a port, the nurses are starting to say. I want to shake them for giving her one more magic procedure, one more hope. But it's not my body and these are not my decisions. I keep my mouth shut, make more appointments, do more tests, give more medications. She does whatever the doctors say.

The timer goes off and I return to the TV room to lift the wet towel from her leg and apply a fresh dressing. She asks for an English muffin with cream cheese. I bring it to her along with a glass of orange juice.

"I need to eat something before I take my pills," she says. "You do so much for me, dear. Thank you."

On the morning show, one of the hosts has traveled someplace warm and wide, with white beaches slipping out to great swaths of blue.

"Guess I'll get back in my bed," Jeanne says, handing me her half-finished plate. "Don't know why I'm so worn out today."

Just before she clicks off the TV, the programming cuts to the local weather report. Storms possible tomorrow—

Jeanne pushes her walker down the hall toward her bedroom, and the clear tubing trails and tangles behind her. Her oxygen concentrator hums and gasps.

Jeanne gets a mammogram every October. This year when the postcard came in the mail, I encouraged her to let it slide.

"Mom, before we call and schedule the appointment, think about it. You always say how painful it is, how you dread it."

"But if I have breast cancer—"

"If there's a spot, you'll return for more tests. A biopsy would create another wound that won't heal. And if you do have breast cancer, what are you going to do—surgery? Radiation and chemo?" This is a woman who scratches an itch on her arm and ends up with a wound that doesn't heal for weeks.

"You're right, Lisa. Even if I had cancer I wouldn't want treatment. But at least I'd know."

"That's fair, Mom. But think about it, will you?"

Protocol: mammogram every year after forty. That's what the brochures say. How likely is it that Jeanne would live long enough to die of breast cancer?

We think one step at a time. Ease the breathing. Take the prednisone. When her skin starts breaking down because of poor circulation, we apply ointment and bandages. Blood samples are taken and corpuscles counted. Radiologists interpret x-rays and CT scans. Jeanne spends her time in doctors' offices, in labs, in the hospital, when she could be watching the hibiscus grow and blossom red in the backyard; she could be reading books to her grandchildren.

After two days she threw the postcard away. I wasn't the one making the decision, but my influence was clear. Jeanne doesn't question medical advice enough—I question it too much. I hope I'm not wrong to dissuade her from treatment. I'm relieved to let the yearly mammogram go. If nothing else, there is one less possibility of her falling while getting from wheelchair to car and back again.

When Dr. Rubin asked if she'd scheduled her mammogram, I felt a rush of shame. Maybe I was wrong. She explained to him why she decided to forgo it. He nodded, wrote in her chart, said nothing at all.

❁

Autumn comes late to North Texas. The girls go trick-or-treating in sandals most years. By Thanksgiving the nights are cool and it's time to prune back for winter. This is the only time of year that gardening is any fun for me. In the spring and summer we have fire ants and beastly heat. But the late fall in Texas is moderate and the gardening is more my style—all about tidying up and getting rid rather than planting and coaxing and cajoling.

Todd's no gardener, either. The first two years we lived here, we got pink notes taped to our door every few months from some member of the homeowner's association, letting us know that our weeds were an inch above the window ledge—a height forbidden by the covenant we signed when we moved into this community. Todd bought a weed whip and kept the weed height in check until we could hire a landscaper to put in a decent front bed for us. We budgeted extra to have one corner of the backyard landscaped. Jeanne's bay window looks out to that corner of the yard, where red hibiscus surrounds the trunk of a bald cypress, and the dark pink blossoms of autumn sage draw hummingbirds and butterflies.

I dump the uneaten bit of English muffin into the disposal, load the dishwasher, and dry my hands. Now that she's back in bed I can get things done without feeling like I'm neglecting her. I've been meaning to prune the back garden, where the low-growing autumn sage bushes have become spindly from lack of care. No reason to put off the task any longer.

The pruning shears I left on the porch last summer have become rusty, but when I open-close them, I find they will still cut. I recently learned that I should have been clipping back the hibiscus all season to maximize blossoms. Now the worn-out stalks stretch in all directions, reaching and bending low, unable to support their own weight. I cut back a big stem nearly my height.

In the drought of summer, while the rest of the yard went to hay, I hand-watered this section of the yard so Jeanne could enjoy the view. I put up a leaky hummingbird feeder and refilled it with sugar water every few days for the one green-throated fellow who hovered and delighted Jeanne—but I didn't prune anything. I didn't know that I should. After her cataract surgery, Jeanne said the colors of the overgrown hibiscus and autumn sage were brilliant.

A light breeze lifts my hair from my shoulders as I cut every hibiscus plant back to the ground. I've read that they'll rise again in spring, but that's really hard to believe. What if I've misunderstood? But it's too late now to change my mind. I rake all the clippings and toss them into the fenced side yard where we compost.

The autumn sage bushes look scrappy now that their hibiscus backdrop is gone. The sage, too, should have been trimmed through the growing season—should have been kept close to the ground so the internal growth didn't become woody. I prune one-third—maybe more—from each bush. What's left is blossomless and lonely against the bare garden that was moments ago a tangle.

I glance toward the bay window. The shades are up, so I can see Jeanne's sleeping shape in bed. My scalp prickles and my neck feels suddenly cold. It's not yet winter, but here I am rushing autumn to an end.

❁

For lunch I make sandwiches—grilled cheese with applesauce on the side, her favorite—and we sit together to eat.

"I see you've pruned back for winter," Jeanne says.

"Oh, Mom, it's so sad to lose the blossoms and say good-bye to the growth."

She takes a bite of her sandwich while looking out the window, appraising my work.

"Well," she says. "It is getting toward winter."

Outside our kitchen window, clouds cushion the sky in variegated grays.

Her Choice

Pussycat Mew jumped over a coal
And in her best petticoat burnt a great hole
Poor pussy's weeping, she'll have no more milk
Until her best petticoat's mended with silk

Nursery rhyme

It's January again. One year since Jeanne started the infusions and two since she stopped smoking. We return to the immunologist.

"Do you feel better, Mrs. Harris. Are the treatments helping?"

"Oh, yes, so much."

I speak up—something I didn't do six months ago when we were here. "She has lung infections every four weeks now—more often now than before she started the infusions."

"I see," he says. "Well, it doesn't work for everyone."

Jeanne speaks up, "I'm afraid that if I don't have the infusions I'll get even worse."

"Well, I'll tell you this," the doctor says. "Medicare does not like to pay for these treatments—they're expensive, several thousand dollars each time. If Medicare asks me, I will have to say that your condition is unchanged, and Medicare won't continue to pay. However, as long as the insurance company doesn't inquire about improvement, this is a decision I like to leave to the patient. It's your call, Mrs. Harris."

Jeanne looks at her hands. Her right wrist is badly bruised from the last infusion, when the nurse had a hard time getting into the vein. All the hours spent in the clinic, the lost days while she recovers from exhaustion.

Jeanne says, "I want the infusions."

"Okay, Mrs. Harris." He closes her file. "See you in six months."

I lower my head against the January wind as I push the wheelchair across the parking lot.   Once Jeanne is in the passenger's seat, I place the oxygen tank on the floor by her feet and shut the door, careful not to catch the tubing.

Near the freeway entrance a homeless woman stands in the cold. She looks about twenty. I reach to the backseat with one arm, feeling for the pair of too-small gloves Todd received as a Christmas gift from one of his students. I ask Jeanne to roll down her window as we wait at the light, and I push the gloves into her lap. "Give her these, and the bag of trail mix from my purse."

"Here, *Miss!*" I call through the window. The young woman's eyes meet mine as she steps close to the car. She smiles, showing decayed teeth. "God bless you," she says. "Thanks."

More than five thousand dollars in human blood product is poured into Jeanne's delicate veins each month. How much would the dental work cost to fix this homeless woman's mouth? What would it take to get her into an apartment and off the side of the road?

As the light changes to green, the woman slips the gloves into her pocket. They are hers now—not for me to legislate whether she uses them. Maybe she knows from experience that on a frigid day she'll have more success panhandling with bare hands. Or perhaps she'll sell the gloves for a few dollars, use the money for a drink or a hit—an hour of escape from feeling the chill wind.

The light changes and I follow the cars ahead of us to the freeway on-ramp, merge, and head southeast, toward home.

Jeff and Genevieve

As round as an apple, as deep as a cup
And all the king's horses can't fill it up

Nursery rhyme

"*Mom was coughing a lot when I called,*" Jeff says. "She sounded awful."

I tell Jeff how discouraged I've been since the nosebleed and subsequent decline and how I feel torn between Jeanne's doctors and Jeanne's wishes. If she has another nosebleed, can I take her at her word that she wants to stay home and bleed to death?

"Sounds like we're stuck between two paradigms," Jeff says. "A life-saving doctor can't understand why someone would decide at the end of her life that she doesn't want to experience any more pain, even in exchange for more time."

I complain to Jeff as freely as I do with Todd. Jeff comforts me and counsels me—he is more than an in-law; he's a friend and a brother. For all the anguish and discontent of my life with Jeanne, through caring for her I have gained such closeness with Jeff.

"They're flying me out to interview, Lisa." Jeff's talking about a university just an hour or so north of Fort Worth. "I think I'll have an offer within a week. I'll need to look at real estate, at a school for Gen. If it all goes smoothly, I'll be there to help with Mom in the fall. I want to be there for you guys like you've been there for me and Gen since Carolyn died."

"Just let us know what we can do to help," I say.

"I have to nail this interview," Jeff says. "First things first."

Jeff has realized he needs to leave Hawaii, where everything is saturated with memories of Carolyn. It's amazing that his job search has resulted in a strong possibility so close to us and Jeanne. It's a new beginning for Jeff, a bright future after such heavy loss.

Her Best Friend's Funeral

O mourner, O mourner, you must believe
Going home in the chariot in the morning

Negro spiritual

In late February, on the day of her best friend's funeral, Jeanne wakes with a severe backache.

"All across my hips," she says. "I can't think what I did to bring this on. Oh, I didn't want to miss Levearn's funeral."

"You are going to this funeral," I tell her. "Take Darvocet."

I bring her the bottle of pink narcotic tablets, and she takes one.

"I'll get you up in an hour, Mom. Plenty of time to get dressed and drive over to the church."

"Thank you, dear. I think it feels better already."

I leave Jeanne's in-law suite and call Todd on his cell. "Your mom's back is hurting." I tell him how I bossed her to take the painkiller, how I insisted that she must go to this funeral.

"Good," Todd says. "You're wise, Lisa."

A month or so ago, I overheard Jeanne on the phone, saying, "I want to see Levearn, but Lisa just won't take me." Jeanne was weak from pneumonia and still taking antibiotics at that time, but her caller must have thought I was the bad guy.

An hour after dosing the Darvocet, I wake Jeanne and plug in her curling iron. I select a blouse and slacks, and I lock the wheelchair into place in the bathroom. She sits there while buttoning her blouse and fixing her makeup.

"My back feels better," Jeanne says. "It really does."

Her hair looks awful from behind—all flattened in a whorl pushed to one side from the pressure of her head on the pillow. Jeanne applies her own makeup, a cream foundation that clumps in her pores. She puts on her blush and lipstick, and all the while I attempt to get her hair to lie flat—with water, the blow dryer, the curling iron, the hairspray. From the front it looks nice enough.

Jeanne and Levearn were part of what they liked to call the "famous foursome." Together with Virginia and Barb, these four old ladies ran the church, their minister liked to joke. When Levearn learned that one church member couldn't afford to heat her apartment in winter, the four-some took turns delivering groceries and taking special cash offerings for an anonymous need. The foursome took a blow when Barb got lung cancer and began to receive hospice care in her home. Nine months later the group was down to three. Then Jeanne's emphysema worsened and it seemed she would be the next to go, until Levearn was admitted to the hospital with amyloidosis, a disease that would soon destroy her kidney function.

In September, during Levearn's first weeks of hospitalization, Jeanne had cataract surgery. I helped put four kinds of drops in each eye daily for six weeks. By mid-October her vision was no longer dimmed by cataracts, but her trifocals weren't the right prescription for her surgically improved eyes. The doctor said her eyes were still changing and that she must wait until November for new glasses. Once her eyes were healed, she would go visit Levearn, Jeanne said. In the meantime, the doctor suggested reading glasses, just the cheap kind from the drugstore. I took her to Walgreens—without bringing the oxygen tank—and we walked to the glasses display.

There in the back of the store Jeanne became short of breath, pursing her lips the way the physical therapist had taught her in pulmonary rehab. The color left her cheeks. Just down the aisle stood a small plastic table. I grabbed it.

"Here, Mom, sit and catch your breath." The skin around Jeanne's lips was turning bluish green, what the nurses called *dusky*.

"Good thought, dear," she said. "A minute or two. I'll be fine." The table was low—lower than she had realized—and she sat down hard. The table legs splayed outward like Bambi slipping on the ice. One of them broke off entirely as the table collapsed, and Jeanne fell to the floor, flat on her back.

"Oh, Mom—" I knelt down and put my hand under her head, like a pillow. "Are you okay?"

"Nothing feels broken, dear."

"I'm sorry. I'm so sorry."

Jeanne was calm. She looked me in the eye—no accusation there, only trust.

"Things do happen. Question is—how do I get up?" From the end of the aisle, a mother and her two small children stared at us. I moved around Jeanne and shielded her from their gaze.

"Can you get into a crawling position and stand up from there?"

"I'm sure I don't have the strength in my legs. Maybe if you bring me the shopping cart I can pull myself up on that."

"I don't think that's a good idea, Mom."

A sturdy Walgreens employee came rushing down the aisle, quickly squatted, grasped Jeanne from behind in something like a Heimlich position, then lifted. He didn't even ask first—just jumped to action. Once she was upright and still in his grasp, Jeanne's legs flailed for the ground. He held her steady until she found her footing.

"Forget the reading glasses, Mom. Let's get you to the car." I held her hand as we walked slowly back through the aisles, out the automatic doors, and down the step from the pavement to the parking lot. She rested one hand on the car, huffing, as I unlocked the passenger's door.

Not many weeks later she fell again—first in her bathroom, and then again late at night in the TV room. By the time her eyes healed and her vision was restored, she had become too frail to drive. I took her wherever she needed to go, whether to doctor appointments, church meetings, hospital visits, or her best friend's funeral.

When Levearn was diagnosed, Jeanne braced herself. Amyloidosis has no cure. From the onset of the disease to death is a matter of months. Levearn's family insisted that every treatment be administered, every effort be made to keep her alive a few weeks more in the ICU. Virginia drove to the hospital daily to spend a few hours with Levearn, each evening calling Jeanne to update her. As a registered nurse, Virginia may have understood more than Levearn's family did about the situation, but she didn't feel free to speak her mind—until she phoned Jeanne. The two left of the famous foursome were troubled that no one was willing to tell their friend she was dying. No one asked Levearn what *she* wanted.

Early in December Jeanne's minister called. I could tell from the one-sided conversation that Betsy was planning a pastoral call to see Levearn in the hospital, and she wanted to know if Jeanne would like to come along. In the few moments of that phone conversation I imagined the beginning of more opportunities for a new kind of social life. Once her friends realized she now needed rides and help getting around, offers would come. Jeanne would get out without me along as her chauffeur and private nurse.

"No thanks, Betsy. Lisa will see about me." A little small talk and the call was over.

"Mom," I said, "why not let Betsy take you? She can push the wheelchair as well as I can."

"I don't want to trouble her," Jeanne said. "No one realizes how much help I need."

But Virginia knew. Jeanne made her promise not to tell church friends how bad it was. Virginia could say only that Jeanne was still under the weather, that she was going through a rough patch and would be back soon.

Virginia pushed back, lightly. "But it's hard for me, Jeanne. It's not quite right. I feel like I'm lying to them."

Not long after that, Jeanne had a question for me.

"Do you think I'm housebound?" she asked.

Without my help out to the car, without me to push the wheelchair, Jeanne certainly was stuck in the house. Didn't that make her housebound? When Todd offered to take her somewhere, she nearly always found a reason to turn him down: for some reason, Jeanne only wanted me.

"Betsy said she would put me on the prayer list for housebound members," she continued.

I felt like thanking Betsy. Maybe if the church people knew how frail Jeanne was they would reach out to her more.

"I'm not like Ann Malcolm, who doesn't even know where she is half the time," Jeanne said. "Or Harold Steel, who was a cranky misfit long before he went into the nursing home. If I'm on the housebound list, I'll get lumped in with those people."

"Mom, people would come visit you if they knew. I feel sure of that."

"Tell me, then, do *you* think I'm housebound?"

I never did answer her question, but I told her what she wanted to hear.

"Mom, you can just tell Betsy to leave you off the prayer list."

"Well, I already did."

One rainy day just after Christmas, Virginia came to our home directly from the hospital, where Levearn's family wanted to ask the doctor about a pacemaker so Levearn could "get better" from her terminal condition.

Virginia took a slow sip of her tea, then said, "Levearn will not be coming home." I could hear the rain outside as I waited for one of them to speak.

Setting her mug down on the coffee table, Virginia asked, "Now, Jeanne, how are you feeling?"

Jeanne reported that she was tired from the pneumonia but breathing better. Virginia remarked that the lung infections seemed more frequent than they used to be. Jeanne didn't think so. She changed the subject to some church gossip.

When Virginia jangled her keys and stood to leave, I walked her down the driveway, slick as it was from the rain. At the car she leaned close to me and said, "Please, if anything happens with Jeanne call me right away."

"I'll call you," I said, thinking she meant another pneumonia.

Virginia sat in the driver's seat, put her keys in the ignition, and said, "One day the antibiotics aren't going to work anymore." Virginia looked up at me. "She'll get a resistant pneumonia. It might be fast."

Virginia kept her eyes on mine.

"When it happens, Lisa, I want to know."

"Okay," I whispered.

I stood alone by the curb as Virginia drove away.

When we'd seen Dr. Rubin in mid-November about Jeanne's falls and resulting leg wound, he'd assigned a visiting nurse to check the wound three times a week. Meanwhile, Levearn started dialysis, was released from the hospital, then fell and was admitted again the next day. Jeanne got pneumonia. I dashed out for groceries when I could and made sure I was home most of the time to fix meals for Jeanne and to answer the door when the nurse came. In December I helped Jeanne choose her Christmas gifts online and placed the order. Then the kids were out of school for the winter holidays. I was secretly glad for an excuse not to visit Levearn. When my children were small, I could hold a toddler's hand in a bumpy parking lot and keep her from falling. I could lift an infant out of her car seat and swing her into the stroller. With my new charge, the task was not so easy.

At the same time, there is something comforting, almost empowering, in knowing how to dress a wound, in being able to recognize symptoms of a dangerous respiratory infection even before Jeanne realizes she is short of breath. I've become an excellent caregiver, and along the way I'm the one who has created the illusion that she doesn't need anyone else.

Finally, one January evening, we drove to the hospital to see Levearn. In the parking lot I opened the back of the minivan and lifted out the wheelchair, a lightweight transport model with small rear wheels.

When I pulled the tailgate of the van closed, the wheelchair rolled away behind me and I had to dash to keep it from hitting a parked car. I pushed it back to Jeanne's door and locked the wheels. Jeanne handed me her purse and then the oxygen tank. I untangled the tubing from her feet.

In one movement she slid out of the passenger's seat, pivoted, and let her body fall into the seat of the wheelchair. Jeanne's weight coming down suddenly tipped the chair, and it began to go over backward. The front wheels were both off the ground when I caught one of the armrests in my free hand—holding her oxygen tank and purse in the other—and somehow I kept her from tipping and pulled the front wheels back down to the ground.

My heart pounded. How hard would the impact have been when her head hit the pavement? I should have been standing behind the wheelchair, steadying it as she sat down. Why hadn't I noticed that we were parked on an incline?

We didn't say anything for a few moments. Jeanne was pale when she asked, "Do we go on to see Levearn or do we go back home?"

"I have got to brace the wheelchair when you sit," I said, upset with myself. "I've got to remember." More silence. "We're here. Let's go see Levearn."

I pushed the wheelchair into the hospital and down the hall to intensive care, where Levearn lay confused and thin and weak. No color in her face and no sparkle in her eyes.

Jeanne held Levearn's hand. I chased down a nurse and asked for ice chips and a spoon. When I returned to the room I stroked Levearn's hair like I do for my girls when they are sick or scared.

"I just want to go home," Levearn said. "It's not comfortable here."

"Don't worry, dear," Jeanne said. "You'll be better soon."

I stared hard at Jeanne, trying to catch her eye. Here was our chance to speak the truth to Levearn. But Jeanne wouldn't meet my eyes. She said what she was supposed to say, even though she felt as strongly as Virginia did that someone should speak the truth.

"We'll get you home, Levearn," Jeanne promised.

Weeks later, Levearn's obituary would be published in the local paper: *On February 18, Levearn O'Malley went home to be with Jesus.*

On the drive back from the hospital, Jeanne told me a friend from church had called that afternoon. She used the word *nag* to describe his concern about getting her to come back to church.

"He just doesn't get it," she said.

"Mom, if this guy wants to see you back at church, maybe he's the first person to ask for help. Surely he would be glad to offer you a ride."

"But he can't just honk the horn and expect me to come running out the door. They don't realize."

"You have to tell people you need help," I said. "I know it's hard. It takes humility."

She didn't think it was pride that kept her from asking. She said it was fear. What happens if the wheelchair goes over backward on someone else's watch? Or if she trips?

I suspect that Jeanne's real fear is that her friends might see how weak she's become, how diminished.

"We know each other's bodies," Jeanne said to me. "When you hold my hand, you feel it—whether I need to slow down or if I start to lose my balance. We work well together."

I couldn't argue with her. But well matched as we are, I have grown weary of our performances as puppet and puppeteer.

Five minutes before the funeral we pull into the church parking lot to find the handicapped parking space taken—no surprise, in this church with so many elderly members. I spot two empty spaces, adjoining, and park in one of them, the other giving me room for the wheelchair.

"How's your back?" I ask.

"The Darvocet's working," Jeanne says. "I really do need to be here. I need this closure. Thank you so much."

"I loved Levearn, too," I say. But Jeanne doesn't hear me. She's already waving to ladies across the parking lot, sitting a little straighter in the wheelchair as we make our entrance. On this day I will take Jeanne where she needs to go, and I won't resent my role. I will greet and smile and shake hands and say *it's no trouble at all.*

At the handicapped ramp I lower my body slightly to get my shoulders into the shove I need to push the wheelchair up onto the pavement near the church entryway.

Friends greet Jeanne as if she's a celebrity. *So good to see you!—You look wonderful!—There's that smile we love!* I stand behind the wheelchair, pushing her forward in six-inch increments as she greets her public.

I maneuver Jeanne's wheelchair next to the end of one of the rows and lock it in place before walking back to the rear of the church to collect a couple of programs from an usher. As I return up the aisle, Jeanne is speaking with the choir director. She gestures and laughs, throwing her head back. Her hair still looks awful, and suddenly I see Jeanne the way everyone else sees her. She is a frail old lady acting competent and important, but it's not news to anyone that she needs a caregiver and a driver and help with the wheelchair. Her friends all maintain the illusion just as much as I do.

Virginia comes up beside me in the aisle and I turn to her. We embrace, and Virginia's shoulders heave against mine, then stiffen as she draws her body erect and pulls out of the hug. Virginia meets my eyes, looks away. We both know.

This is the church where we'll have Jeanne's funeral. Betsy will preach the homily. Virginia will be here, the last one left. I will sit in the front row and play the part of the grieving daughter-in-law, with my back turned to Jeanne's audience.

Zelda

Hector Protector was dressed all in green
Hector Protector was sent to the queen
The queen did not like him
No more did the king
So Hector Protector was sent back again

Nursery rhyme

The home health aide is late on this, her first day with us. It's a bad omen, if you believe in that sort of thing. Jeanne is nervous and I want this transition to go smoothly—the aide's tardiness doesn't boost my confidence, or Jeanne's.

It's been two full weeks since I gave Jeanne a shower. *Two weeks.* But she's been so weary and sleeping and I've been busy with kids, homework, meals, I don't even know what. She can no longer risk stepping into the shower without help. With clenched teeth I say under my breath, *I can't do it all.* Sure, I'm busy, but I've let her go two weeks without a shower. There's no excuse for that. When Dr. Rubin suggested a shower aide from home health and said Medicare would pay the cost, I felt such relief.

Once while I lathered her shampoo Jeanne went blue around the lips, and by the time I realized it and unkinked the clear oxygen tubing so she could breathe, I felt sick to my stomach. Often Jeanne doesn't feel any symptoms when her oxygen drops. She could have passed out, naked on the shower stool, fallen to the hard tile, and what would I have done? After that I made sure the phone was nearby when I gave her a shower, which was less and less often. And now, an aide from home health.

Late the first day isn't good, but when the aide arrives I'm pleased that she is sharp-looking, well mannered, professional. Her name is Zelda. I show Zelda back to the in-law suite, where Jeanne waits.

"The towels are on the shelf," I say. "I use one to line the walker seat and one for her hair. The rags are here, and this soap is more gentle on her skin." Zelda helps Jeanne remove her housedress.

"Turn the water on first. This bathroom is a long way from the hot water heater, and if you undress her before you turn the water on she'll have to sit a long time in the cold." I hear how bossy I sound, as if I know best. I don't wait but step past Zelda and turn the shower water on—all the way hot.

I can't seem to stop. I tell Zelda about the terrycloth robe, how to help Jeanne put it on when she's dripping wet so the robe can dry her. Zelda smiles politely and nods. She pulls on latex gloves.

I say I can't be responsible for all of Jeanne's care, yet here I am micro-managing. Somehow I have to learn to let go.

Zelda gently takes Jeanne's glasses off and lays them on the bathroom counter. The lenses are filthy. I joke about cataract surgery doing no good when she wears glasses this thick with dust.

"Here, I'll wash these for you, Mom."

Only I don't wash them there in the bathroom. I take them out to the kitchen.

I'm torn. I know I'm pushing, but Zelda might screw up. Who says Jeanne won't fall with Zelda in there? Zelda doesn't seem as concerned about safety as I am. I should watch this first time. If she does something really wrong I can at least let home health know.

Who have I become?

At the kitchen sink I wash the glasses slowly, carefully. Hot water does better than cold, so I wait for the water to warm up before I swish each lens through, apply a squeeze of liquid soap, then gently rub away the dust and grime. With a soft rag I dry them, hold them up to the light coming through the kitchen window, wipe away a stubborn smear, and walk back to the in-law suite. The double doors to the bathroom are wide open.

Jeanne sits on the walker seat, naked. Her nose is dripping and she stretches her hand vaguely for the tissue box just out of reach on the bathroom counter. Zelda stands beside her, one hand in the water, testing the temperature. She should be watching Jeanne's face, anticipating her needs. What if next time it's not a drippy nose but a lack of balance—or the dusky greenish blue around her lips when her oxygen drops?

Jeanne bows her head and swipes her nose with the back of her hand, then wipes it on the towel. She rests her head on her hand and looks at the floor.

Quietly, I lay her glasses on the bedside table and leave the room.

Stockpiling

And when she was bad she was horrid

Nursery rhyme

"*I'm low on heart pills* and I need more Darvocet."

Jeanne and I are making a list of prescriptions to be renewed by Dr. Rubin.

"Mom, you have lots of Darvocet."

"No, I'm almost out. The leg pain at night—sometimes I need a second pill, but Dr. Rubin only wants me to take one."

The last time she asked Dr. Rubin about a Darvocet prescription, he told her she still had more than sixty pills left. He knew exactly.

"I think he'll authorize two pills per night if you tell him, Mom. But you still have a good supply."

"Oh, no. Those doctors are very protective of their narcotics."

I add Darvocet to the list. When I finish my coffee, I leave Jeanne to her TV watching and I slip back to the in-law suite's bathroom. I feel as if I'm stealing cookies as I pull from her towel cupboard the plastic bins where she keeps her medications. Sure enough. Two substantial bottles of Darvocet from the mail-order pharmacy. I open the heavier bottle and it is filled to the brim with pink tablets. I dump them out and count, stopping when I reach one hundred. I find another bottle maybe one-third full of Darvocet. With both in hand, I return to Jeanne's TV room.

"Look, Mom, I found some Darvocet."

She stiffens. "Yes. Those are leftovers."

I sit on her footstool so we are more or less eye to eye. "You don't have to stock up, Mom. He's not going to withhold pain medication."

"I need a new prescription. These pills are just extras to have on hand. He doesn't know about them."

"Jeanne," I say. I seldom call her by name. "He knows. He won't write the scrip for you."

"I'll manage my own medicines," she says. "Don't you trust me?"

"Mom, we're not going to ask for more Darvocet."

I'm looking her in the eye, this woman who raised my husband, who has a master's degree. And she's wrong. I am right.

To Sleep, to Dream

Donkey, donkey, old and gray
Ope your mouth and gently bray
Lift your ears and blow your horn
To wake the world this sleepy morn

Nursery rhyme

"Mom? Mom, wake up."

It's midafternoon and Jeanne has been sleeping all day. I say her name loudly. She sleeps on. I put my hand on her shoulder and shake her, hard. Jeanne mumbles that she's so tired but doesn't open her eyes. She has always told me not to call the ambulance. She's not in distress. Do I need to do anything?

The phone rings. A callback from Debbie, the pulmonologist's nurse. She tells me not to worry, that when oxygen levels get too low, the patient can slip into a deep sleep and be hard to rouse. Dr. Fletcher isn't in the office.

"I can't advise you, Lisa, but it sounds to me like low oxygen—hypoxia. I know your mother doesn't want to be intubated. Is she comfortable?"

"She seems to be. But will I get in trouble—legally, I mean—if I don't call an ambulance?"

"Oh, no, you won't get in trouble," Debbie says. "You know she doesn't want to be intubated. She's comfortable, right? Don't we all wish we could die in our sleep?"

I ask Debbie what to do if Jeanne becomes short of breath or scared. She says Ativan helps, and morphine, but those are really only available with hospice.

"Hospice, really?" I ask. "Will Dr. Fletcher give a referral or something?"

"Oh, he doesn't like hospice," Debbie tells me. "He thinks it makes patients give up."

Just a week ago Dr. Fletcher signed papers for one of his patients to be admitted to hospice. The patient died the next day. Debbie tells me this as if it were proof that hospice kills patients. My only thought is that if the patient died one day after entering hospice, then he got the hospice care too late.

"Try boosting her oxygen up a liter or so," Debbie recommends. "See if that peps her up." Debbie also suggests I call the home health nurse to come check Jeanne's oxygen saturation and give a listen to her heart. We would still not be obligated to call an ambulance, but then we'd have a better feel for whether or not she's hypoxic. "Maybe it's a flu virus or something," Debbie says. "Let me know how it goes, will you?" We say good-bye.

I turn up the dial on the oxygen concentrator, and forty-five minutes later the home health nurse arrives. As soon as the nurse and I enter the room, Jeanne wakes. Her heart is fine, her breathing is fine. Her oxygen saturation is okay at 91 percent, but the nurse encourages Jeanne to use the nebulizer, to open the lungs and help her take in more oxygen.

Jeanne gets up to do a breathing treatment when the nurse leaves. She asks me to bring her a Diet Coke. When she turns the nebulizer off, I repeat what Debbie said about hypoxia.

"Jeanne, I need to know what you want. If you fall into a very deep sleep because your oxygen levels are dropping, do you want me to call the ambulance?" She does not.

"Lisa, I really don't feel like I'm dying."

Probably I am overreacting.

❀

Two more days pass, with Jeanne sleeping most of the time and reporting that she feels "weak as a kitten." Todd and I talk as if this is the end; we call Todd's brothers and Uncle Harry to let them know. We wonder what we should say to the girls. Jeanne seems totally at peace. She says, "If this is an end-of-life thing, I hope it doesn't go on too much longer."

Todd confesses that he's starting to send out job inquiries to other schools. "I'll get you back to the Northwest," Todd pledges. "Get our girls some wilderness to explore."

It's a false promise, I know, but so sweet I tear up.

"I mean it, Lisa. I've already sent out my résumé." Todd tells me about a school in Washington State, two more in Oregon, all looking for an administrator.

I can't get my hopes up, because the only way we could move is if Jeanne dies. I tell Todd that even if Jeanne is at the end of her life, there's no way we could pack everything, fix up the house and find a buyer, and move across the country all before fall. Not possible, I tell him. Besides, Jeff expects a job offer any day now. Won't we be abandoning him if we move away?

Todd tells Jeff what we're thinking. Jeff says that's okay, the job here is best for his career and he's not taking it just to be closer to us. He tells Todd he knows that we'll move away once Jeanne is gone.

I go back and forth from hour to hour thinking yes, she's dying, and then no, I'm assuming the worst and she just has a bug. But doesn't a bug usually come along with symptoms?

I ask Jeanne a couple of times each day if she wants to go to the emergency room. So far she has said no, but today she says she might change her mind. Just not yet.

❖

Jeff calls to ask how I'm holding up.

"It's easy. She sleeps all the time, Jeff. I just wish we knew."

"Lisa, whether this is 'it' or not, Mom is near the end of her life. She keeps getting pneumonia. Old people die from pneumonia. They keep seeing spots on her lungs. Smoke for fifty years and you just might get lung cancer. We are in the last years if not months."

"I just don't want to cause her death by my negligence—by not taking her to the doctor when I should."

Jeff tells me about Carolyn's hospitalization, how she filled out paperwork after the diagnosis. *Where do you want to die?* Carolyn checked the box for *at home*. But she was hooked up to a half-dozen tubes and wires. Stage IV cancer with no hope of treatment. Jeff remembers seeing those checked boxes and thinking, *How the hell do I get you home?*

"Don't take her to the hospital, Lisa. Once she gets started on tests and procedures it's hard to check back out of the system. She says she doesn't want that. Stay home."

When I say Jeanne doesn't think she's dying, Jeff laughs and says, "Yeah, well, how would she know what it feels like? She's never died before."

✿

One of the schools in Oregon schedules a phone interview with Todd. He gets off the phone grinning. "I think it went really well," he says. "This could be the one."

The school is in Newberg, a small town an hour and a half from my parents and brothers. I stayed there once in college when I attended a conference at George Fox University. I remember filbert orchards and fall colors. "Newberg would be perfect," I say. So perfect it scares me. What if Todd gets this job and we rush Jeanne to her death in order to move on with our lives?

"I think they're going to fly me out for an interview," Todd says. "They would want me in place by July 1."

Could we possibly sell the house, pack our stuff, be ready to move to Oregon in June? And Jeff and Genevieve are moving to Texas in August— they plan to stay with us the first couple of weeks. I look around at Jeanne's knickknacks and furniture and paintings, and I think about her boxes in the garage, her stockpiles in the closets of the in-law suite. I remember the taste of blackberries in August, the sound of gentle rain falling on Douglas fir, the smell of the ocean.

✿

"Oh, I'm so short of breath," Jeanne says through the mist from the nebulizer.

"Did you cough in the night?"

She shakes her head.

"Any tightness in your chest? Back pain?"

"No. Just can't catch my breath."

I hear gunk scrabbling in her chest with every breath. This is new. I mention that early morning is a great time to go to the emergency room—the crowds don't start until after nine.

"Maybe Dr. Fletcher can get you admitted directly. Then we'd avoid the ER and just get you a room and medicine and breathing treatments."

"I have all that at home," she says. And she's right. But I'm scared. A deep, comfortable sleep is one thing, but this shortness of breath and no way for me to monitor her oxygen levels or to relieve distress—this doesn't feel right. Suddenly I don't want her to die at home, especially not if she's gasping for breath. I want her in a hospital. I want it to be someone else's responsibility. I've already let this go too long, just calmly waiting for her to die. What was I thinking? If I'd taken her to the doctor last week, it wouldn't have gotten to this point. I'm denying medical treatment. I'm like those death doctors. I may as well inject her with something.

"Okay, Mom, I can call Dr. Fletcher's office at 9:00 and ask them to squeeze us in."

"Sounds good, dear. I think I'll just go back to bed for a while."

I call Dr. Fletcher's office. Debbie answers, and I tell her Jeanne needs to be admitted to the hospital, I'm sure of it. Another pneumonia, probably, but she refuses to go to the ER. I want to see if Dr. Fletcher would admit her directly.

"Oh, I'm sorry," says Debbie. "No doctors here today. We're catching up on charts."

"No doctors," I repeat. "Oh. I guess it's the ER, then. If I can convince her to go."

"You know, let me check something. Can I put you on hold?"

After a few minutes, Debbie comes back to the phone and tells me that we can see the physician assistant, Cindy, who can do the hospital admittance for Jeanne.

In the car I mention the hospital, that Cindy can admit her.

"I'm not interested in being admitted to the hospital," Jeanne says. "I just want a big steroid shot to make it easier to breathe."

But I know she'll need to go to the hospital.

At Dr. Fletcher's office I push the wheelchair to the edge of the x-ray booth.

"Can you stand up, Mrs. Harris?" Debbie asks.

"I can stand," Jeanne says. "I'm not wearing a bra."

"Good girl," Debbie says as she positions Jeanne for the x-ray.

Jeanne's blood pressure is 98/70, which seems weirdly low to me, but Debbie simply records the numbers on Jeanne's chart. Her oxygen is 95 percent. How can she be so short of breath with good oxygen sats?

Debbie leaves as Cindy is entering the exam room.

"Well, Mrs. Harris, there's no pneumonia. Your lungs actually look pretty good on the x-ray," Cindy says.

"I'm just so sleepy all the time. And now I'm short of breath."

"Has she changed medicines recently?"

I shake my head.

"No sign of failure on the x-ray," Cindy says. She means heart failure. I've thought of that, too.

Cindy listens to Jeanne's lungs. "You sound awful," Cindy says. "You're wheezing, girl." Cindy's eyes meet mine. She keeps moving the stethoscope around and shaking her head each time she listens.

"I'm concerned about hypoxia," I say.

"We could do a blood gas," Cindy says.

She's talking about taking blood from an artery to measure the levels of oxygen and carbon dioxide.

"I had one of those a year ago," Jeanne says. "Never again."

"I don't blame you," Cindy says. "They can be very painful. I wouldn't want one, either." Her next words are an echo of Debbie's from a few days ago. Hypoxia would be the way to go. Just get sleepier and sleepier and fall into a deep sleep. The websites I surfed this past week all warned "poten-tially life-threatening—get to a doctor immediately." And this is true. But hypoxia could also be the means of a peaceful death at the end of hopes for good health. That's not something the websites say. Without taking your own life, without any real choice except staying home instead of going to the hospital, this is the death to choose.

"I'm wondering if her lungs are giving out," I say. "If maybe we're at the end."

Cindy seems to perk up. She shifts in her seat, "This is exactly what happens when the body gets ready to shut down," she says. "You sleep much more and eat less. Yes, that could well be what's going on here. It's a natural process. So, tell me, Mrs. Harris. Are you ready if that's what it is?"

"Ready if what?" says Jeanne. "I don't understand you."

"Mom, she means if this is your body shutting down, are you ready to die?"

Jeanne nods. No visible emotion. "Oh, yes. I'm ready. The only thing I'm afraid of is being hooked up to a machine."

Cindy said, "That's a valid concern. It's often what happens. I used to work at the hospital and in their ICU are pulmonary patients like you, on ventilators, and they never come off. But it's hard to predict. There are always some patients who surprise us."

"Do you feel like you're dying?"

"No, I don't. But Lisa is really concerned."

I remember Jeff's words. She doesn't know what it feels like.

I ask Cindy what might be wrong with Jeanne. She lists the possibil-ities: heart failure, high carbon dioxide in the blood, electrolytes imbal-anced, anemia.

"Your COPD is quite severe," she says to Jeanne. "This could be your body's way of saying it's time. We can talk about hospice, Mrs. Harris."

"But don't we need a bunch of tests to get her admitted to hospice?" I ask. "Like the blood gas?"

"I'm pretty sure you do," Cindy says. "And if you're comfortable already, you don't really need hospice. What they can give you is morphine, which really does help with the shortness of breath at the end." Cindy continues to explain—incorrectly, I will later learn—that Jeanne would first have to go into the hospital for a night or so to have tests and determine she has less than six months to live. Then we would have to get set up for hospice and have everything in place at home—hospital bed, equipment, supplies—before she could be discharged.

We sit quietly for a few moments while Cindy looks through Jeanne's chart and waits to see if we have any more questions.

"If you're comfortable now, Mrs. Harris," Cindy says, "I suggest you just go home and rest. I'll give you some prednisone to see if that helps. You know, you can buy your own pulse oximeter online, so you'll know when your oxygen sats drop."

"We'll order one today," I say.

Debbie gives Jeanne a steroid injection and hands me a prescription for several days of increased doses of prednisone.

"Let me walk you out to your car," Debbie says. "I can help with that oxygen tank."

In the parking lot, Debbie says, "I just need one of your hugs today, Mrs. Harris." She has certainly never hugged Jeanne before.

On the drive home, Jeanne says, "This is good. I feel peaceful."

I don't say so, but I feel the same way. No more anxiety. Whatever is going to happen is okay. Sure, we don't have hospice, but maybe she's not dying. If she worsens, that's okay, too. I'm not doing anything wrong. I'm still not sure what we should say to the girls.

✿

After six full days of feeling lousy and sleeping all the time, Jeanne finally starts coughing up discolored sputum. Our new pulse oximeter arrives in the mail, and I check Jeanne's oxygen, which is at 93 percent.

"What is it?" she asks.

"Looking good, Mom," I say without telling her the number. Out in the hallway, I tweak the oxygen concentrator up ever so slightly.

Dr. Fletcher, back in the office, prescribes antibiotics. After just two days on the antibiotics Jeanne feels alert and much better. She is not going to die yet.

The school in Newberg offers to fly Todd out for an interview.

"What should I tell them?" Todd agonizes.

"You have to shoot straight," I say. "Tell them your mom is elderly and ill and that you thought she was in her final weeks of life but she recovered."

"You might be right," Todd says. "But it feels so unprofessional."

"It's the truth," I say. "And anyway, by the time she dies they'll have filled this position. At least you can end it with honesty."

"I'll do it," Todd says, and he begins composing the e-mail that closes a door to the future we long for.

Morning Routine

Friday night's dream, on Saturday told
Is sure to come true, be it never so old

Nursery rhyme

"Do you feel well enough to get your own breakfast today, Mom?"

She's sitting in her TV room with the oxygen tubing under her nose and her walker parked next to the chair. She doesn't answer.

I've been fixing her breakfast and bringing it to her for more than a month now—since that sleepy week when we thought she might be dying. Jeanne's been markedly better for days now. She is definitely frail, but not as frail as I have been treating her.

"Mom, we've got instant oatmeal or grits, cold cereal, toast, bagels, English muffins, or eggs."

"Oh, I think I'll just have a bowl of cereal. A small serving."

She has placed her order.

I read in a caregiver pamphlet that it's important to let the patient do as much for herself as she can. The other day she actually asked me to file her nails. I protested. I have never once filed my own nails—I clip them squarely every few weeks when they start to get in my way. She looked so crestfallen that I ended up doing it anyway. The emery board made me shudder like I do when I hear a rake pulled across pavement. How can she not have the strength to file her own nails? How can I not have the strength to say no and mean it?

❋

I lay in the basement guest room bed, wondering if I should get up. Todd had brought me home to meet his parents, and I wanted so badly for them to like me. I heard Jeanne moving around upstairs in the kitchen, the woman with a gentle Texas accent that kept her vowels large and wide even after thirty years in the Midwest. She was friendly and kind to me but didn't seem particularly charmed. I had no clue whether or not I was making a good impression.

I went upstairs to the main level. Jeanne was slicing a banana over a bowl of cornflakes and didn't see me. On the kitchen bar she had set out an oval yellow placemat, a glass of orange juice and creamer of milk, a spoon and napkin—also a syringe with a small bottle of insulin, and a lancet and glucose meter. She finished slicing the banana, and as she set down the cereal bowl on the yellow placemat, I said, "Good morning."

"Oh, good morning, dear. How did you sleep?"

"Fine, thanks."

"Would you like some juice?"

"Sure."

Then Todd's dad came out from the back of the house, and with a cheerful "Good morning!" he sat down on the barstool and tore the wrapping off the lancet. Jeanne set my glass of juice down at the table. Dewey made a small slice in his own finger and squeezed a bead of blood onto the test strip. Once the number registered, he took the cap off the syringe and inserted the needle through the top of the insulin bottle, pulling out his dose.

"Jeanne," he said.

He handed her the needle and unwrapped an alcohol wipe. He rolled up his shirtsleeve and swabbed his arm. Jeanne administered the injection and recapped the needle. She reached out for the creamer and poured milk over her husband's cereal. Maybe she did this so he would get precise calories and sugar grams according to an exacting diabetic menu. Then he said, "Coffee?" and she hurried to take a rewarmed mug of coffee from the microwave. When he'd finished eating, he left his dishes on the placemat and went to find his briefcase and coat. Jeanne cleared and rinsed the dishes, then picked up the scraps of paper and medical supplies. She was putting the placemat away when Dewey said, "See you for dinner," and left through the side door.

I wondered briefly if Todd expected a wife to measure out his cereal, to pour the milk over it for him. To clean up afterward. I finished my juice. The situation had to be governed by the diabetes and not Harris family gender roles. Surely there was something about this vignette that I simply did not understand.

✳

I pour milk straight from the jug into the cereal bowl and place it on a tray to carry in to Jeanne. We're out of bananas, in fact, out of every kind of fruit. Not even juice concentrate in the freezer. Getting to the store has been hard with Jeanne sick and needing care. That's my excuse, anyway.

"Would you like a cup of tea with that?" I ask. Why am I doing this? I think that I want to give her back some independence, and then I keep coddling. It's like a reflex.

"Oh, tea sounds lovely. Thank you, dear."

I return to the kitchen frustrated with myself. But I offered. She didn't demand anything. No fair for me to be sore about this.

Todd gets his own breakfast—maybe because early in our marriage I intentionally did not lay out placemat and bowl and creamer of milk. When we're both up and hungry, he will make a large omelet and split it with me. We each rinse and load our own plates and forks, as do the girls. One of us plops the sauté pan into the dishwasher and we're on with the day.

But life could have gone differently. If we'd married in the '50s, say. Maybe I would have cared for one son, then two, then three, pouring milk and administering medications for all of them, giving and giving of myself all those years until the babies grew up and left home and fixed their own breakfasts in their own homes, scattered across the globe. At that point— just the two of us alone in the house—pouring cereal and slicing a banana for one man instead of four would have been a cinch, dishes quickly whisked off the table before he even left for work. The gesture would have been a small thing, and I would have fixed his breakfast in hopes that one day there would be someone to do the same for me.

Old Woman

All the king's horses and all the king's men
Couldn't put Humpty together again

Nursery rhyme

It's March, the beginning of tornado season in North Texas and the three-month interval since Jeanne's last CT scan. The waiting room in radiology is crowded today, and Kayla has grown bored with her stickers and coloring pages. Jeanne assured me she'd be fine on her own for the scan, and the receptionist promised to call my cell when Jeanne's finished. Kayla and I have wandered out to the main lobby, a huge space with a small snack bar on one side. I buy Kayla a chocolate milk and a cookie and look around for a place to sit.

The atrium-style lobby is open all the way to the sixth floor. Vines climb long planters along the balcony railings from one floor to another, like Nebuchadnezzar's hanging gardens. This is a place of exposure, not intimacy, yet the lobby furniture is arranged in snug groupings: a comfy couch in a lion's den, a cozy loveseat in a fiery furnace. An old woman sits in one of the overstuffed armchairs. She's short, like I am. I lead Kayla to the armchairs, and when I sit down I find that my feet don't even touch the floor.

"Wow. Deep chair for a short lady," I say. The old woman laughs and scoots her walker to one side so I can set my purse down on the ottoman between us.

"Short isn't so bad," she says. "And these chairs are comfortable."

She smiles and her teeth are clean, bright, even. Her smile is the one I've had ever since I got my braces off at sixteen. At her age, such perfection must mean dentures. Her hair, cut in a short bob, is pure white. My great-great-aunt from Sweden had just such a snowy crown. I hope my own hair, white-blond on my wedding day, will bypass salty-peppery tones and go straight to white.

I think about white hair and strong teeth these days. I think about sagging breasts and high blood pressure, too. In my midforties, I'm exactly halfway between braces and dentures. Halfway between natural blond and shades of gray.

✵

Since Jeanne moved in with us I've watched her become an old woman. She now stoops and shuffles and asks the girls to repeat things, louder please.

Most mornings I kneel beside Jeanne's footstool to change the dressing on her slow-healing leg wound from last October's fall, and often my own middle-aged fingers have a hard time peeling the paper wrapper from the gauze pad. How much longer will I be healthy and strong enough to help her? Her legs are pocked with scars and dappled with bruises. The skin hangs as loosely as a crepe veil.

When I took a shower a few nights ago, I bent down to shave my legs and was surprised that the skin over my calves is firm and tight. I wiped the steam from the mirror and was shocked to see life and youth and health. I reel from the mental time travel between intimate care for a seventy-five-year-old body and dwelling in my own body at forty-four.

I've lost track of myself. Wasn't I just a young mother with too many preschoolers? Todd is three and a half years younger than I, so for years it seemed I took back some youth when I married him. Our first child was born when I was thirty. New friends thought I must be joking when I told them my age. I looked younger than Todd, not older, they said.

Kayla goes to preschool on Tuesdays and Thursdays. I try to schedule all Jeanne's medical appointments on those days, to spare Kayla the hours in waiting rooms and doctor's offices. Most mothers of preschoolers are taking their kids to the park in nice weather or volunteering to help with field trips at preschool. Jessica brought home a sign-up sheet for classroom volunteers, and across the top the teacher had written, "Please sign up to help in class at least twice this quarter." I folded the page in half and tucked it in the recycling bin, out of sight. I suppose Jessica's teachers and all the other parents think I'm a shirker. And Jessica asks me sometimes, "Mommy, why don't you ever bring treats to class parties like the other moms?" I'm not the sentimental type, but a thought hits me sometimes: because I'm being a good daughter-in-law, I'm not as good a mommy.

An acquaintance recently asked, "What will you do with your free time when Kayla goes to kindergarten next year?" For me there will be no freedom when all the kids are in school. Jeanne has doctor appointments and needs lab work done, schedules them two and three times a week.

How long until I need a caregiver myself?

❀

"We've been here since early this morning," the old woman says, again shifting her walker. "My husband's having one of those special x-rays."

"My mother-in-law is here for a CT scan, too," I say.

"She's okay?"

"I think so. A routine check of her lungs is all."

Hospital staff and patients find their way around and through the lobby, walking the perimeter from rotating entry door to elevators to radiology wing. A nurse I remember from the radiology desk pushes a large man in a wheelchair. The nurse's eyes meet mine but don't register recognition. Kayla has finished her snack and has chocolate smeared on one cheek. I rub at it with a napkin.

"They think it's back," the old woman says. "Cancer. His bladder this time."

"That's awful. I'm so sorry." What more can I say?

"First time it was in his kidney. Surgery and chemo, just terrible."

I want to tell her that my dad went through chemotherapy, so I know how horrific it is. But my dad lived and his cancer didn't return. It's been nearly twenty years. I remain silent.

"My mother had cancer," she says. "She died of a heart attack, but she had cancer, too. My father had cancer. My sister had cancer."

Cancer, cancer, cancer. Repeat a word enough and it seems to lose meaning.

"Well, there he is now," she says, standing up. I turn and smile at the man approaching us. He has cancer? He looks younger than his wife, surprisingly strong in his Levi's and western shirt. He walks quickly. None of the familiar old-person shuffle. His thick hair is wavy, parted on one side, a lot like Todd's. If the woman hadn't told me he was her husband, I would think he was her son.

He moves the overstuffed chair so she can more easily maneuver her walker, and he winks at Kayla. He has no idea that I know.

"You need to go now and have a good lunch," I say. What I mean is, go and for a few hours forget what might be ahead. Enjoy today, while he's still strong and you don't know for sure. I want to be a minister in robes, raising my hand in benediction: Go in peace.

She pushes her walker carefully and slowly across the lobby; he walks beside with one protective hand on her back. Kayla takes out her stickers and paper, and we sit for a long time while patients and hospital staff continue to hurry around me en route to procedures and diagnoses.

Another Nosebleed

As I walked to myself
And talked to myself
Myself said unto me
Look unto thyself
Take care of thyself
For nobody cares for thee

Nursery rhyme

I'm upstairs in the loft, and no one else is awake yet. I can hear her coughing and coughing. The emergency room doctor said she shouldn't lie flat in bed or the pressure on the blood vessels might cause renewed bleeding. Jeanne sleeps sitting up in her wingback chair.

Yesterday morning she lay in bed with a bloody tissue screwed up her nose and more blood on the bedding. I heard her words from eight months ago, *Never again. I would rather bleed to death.* I felt my legs go soft. Let nature take its course and I imagined I would go to jail for elder abuse, for neglect. How would I wash out all the blood?

We drove to the hospital in silence. I knew she did not want to go and only consented because I was so shaken. The visit only took a couple of hours, and this time they were able to stop the bleeding without epistaxis balloons. She didn't even need morphine. I brought her home with a nasal tampon in one nostril and instructions to use over-the-counter phenyl-ephrine nasal spray to constrict the blood vessels if bleeding started on the other side. At bedtime last night I settled her in a wingback chair with her feet up on a footstool. I woke twice in the night and crept down to check on her. Both times she was asleep and snoring.

She coughs, hard, every few minutes. Isn't the coughing a greater risk than lying flat? The last nosebleed was long ago, and her health is so much worse now. Colonized bacteria in her lungs get the upper hand every few weeks and she takes antibiotics and coughs and coughs. Now she's trying to breathe through one nostril with a tampon shoved up the other one.

When a person bleeds to death, she gets weaker and weaker and then loses consciousness. Instead Jeanne will suffocate from emphysema or die of pneumonia or break her hip the next time she falls, and die in a nursing home with bedsores and infected wounds and bones that won't knit together.

And yet her latest CT scan was completely clear. The old masses and shadows have all resolved and there are no new concerns. Instead of a CT in two or three months, Dr. Fletcher wants one in six months. I suppose the clear CT is good news, but the steady decline of Jeanne's health and loss of independence are so difficult. I honestly never thought she would live long enough to be so frail she needed full-time nursing care.

At one point in the emergency room visit yesterday her eyes grew red and watery.

"Mom, are you sad or just tired?"

She swallowed and wiped a smear of blood from her upper lip.

"Of course I'm sad," she said. "It's not death that scares me. It's the dying."

April Fool

See, see! What shall I see?
A horse's head where his tail should be

Nursery rhyme

"*Good morning,*" *the admissions clerk says.* "You must be the daughter." Funny, how people so often look right past Jeanne now that she's in a wheelchair.

"Actually," I say, "I'm her daughter-*in-law*."

"We just have a few papers to fill out. Her full name is Eugenia Harris? Does she know her Social Security number?"

"You should ask her," I say. Jeanne and I share a look.

The clerk corrects herself by passing the papers across the desk to Jeanne. "You'll be over to surgery in no time." Name, address, Social Security number, insurance cards, signatures. "Now, Mrs. Harris, this is the form that tells us who we may release your information to. I assume you want your daughter listed on the release form?"

"*In-law.* She's my daughter-in-law."

"Oh, that's right. And you're a widow? So you'll want to list your son as next of kin?"

"No. I want my daughter-in-law."

"Oh . . . okay, so . . . her name is?"

"Lisa Harris."

"You don't happen to know her address?"

"Yes, I know her address. It's the same as mine."

Two years ago, when Jeanne made out an advance directive, she named me as her medical power of attorney—the one who would carry out her wish not to be placed on life support in the end. I was the logical choice, the one who knew Jeanne and her medical condition most intimately. She told me she considered me *next of kin*. In legal terms, next of kin is the person most closely related by blood. In Jeanne's case her next of kin would actually be her brother or one of her sons. I am to her, as legal terms go, a *stranger in blood*. This makes me sound as if she should take out a restraining order, rather than leave decisions to me regarding her life and death.

She considers me her daughter, next of kin, though I'm not. I'm often mistaken as Jeanne's daughter, whether I'm pushing her wheelchair or just sitting beside her in a doctor's waiting room. Nurses, doctors, even Jeanne's close friends from church see a resemblance where there is none. They see a certain strength of the chin, a similar curve of the ear. You look so much alike, they say, you and your mother.

❖

At Jeanne's last infusion, three different nurses took turns for forty-five minutes before one of them finally inserted a needle into a thin and slippery vein.

"You really need a port," the nurse said. "Most of our patients have them."

Most of their patients receive frequent chemotherapy, which is hard on the veins. Ports are recommended so that the harsh drugs can quickly diffuse before spending too much time at full strength in any single vein.

We went back to the immunologist. He reminded Jeanne that she might want to consider giving up the infusions. She replied that she felt they did make a difference and she did not want to stop.

"Can I have blood drawn through the port?" Jeanne asked. "It hurts so much every time those nurses poke me."

"Sure you can," the immunologist answered. "Easy."

He scheduled the surgery for April 1.

The port will be surgically installed into her jugular. I have scoured the Internet for the things that might go wrong: slow healing, ulcers, necrosis of the skin over the port, infection just under the skin, blood clots, systemic sepsis.

I feel sure the port is wrong for Jeanne. Yet I feel ashamed, too—as if I'm wishing she won't get better, as if I want to remove her hope. Maybe my motives are selfish. But surgery? More procedures, more days at the hospital, and for what? To spend hours at the outpatient clinic and come home exhausted and sick. To come down with pneumonia or bronchitis or a sinus infection again and again.

"There are a lot of things that can go wrong with a port," I told her. "I've read about nasty infections, Mom."

Jeanne said she was just trying to follow doctor's orders, that I was the one questioning everything and everyone. Who should she listen to—a daughter-in-law or the doctors and nurses?

I reminded her of the immunologist's words, that he had not recommended the port, she had insisted on it against his weak reminder that the treatments do no good.

"Lisa, what is it that you think I should do?"

So I told her what I thought. Her lungs are shot. The infusions are a waste of time and public money and haven't done any good. She looked straight at me with no expression. I felt as if I'd entered a courtroom and made my case clearly for the first time, but the jury was also the defendant, and if I convinced her, then she would get the death penalty.

"Lisa, it seems that we're in opposite corners on this. I thought I had your support in my medical situation."

"Mom, we're only in opposite corners for this one discussion and only because you asked me what I really think. Once you make a decision, I won't argue. I will support you and be in your corner."

I couldn't look straight at her and tell her to stop the tests and needles, to let herself die. These may be the words she needs to hear, but not from me. I am not next of kin.

An advance directive is not as it seems. You sign for *no extraordinary measures* and this feels clear and controlled, once and for all, but end-of-life issues involve a series of small decisions—sneaky ones, with no big drama—and the life support is already established before any one big decision is made.

As the nurses wheel Jeanne off to surgery I feel dread in the small of my back. I wonder if I am in her corner after all. I find myself almost hoping something will go wrong with the surgery or recovery, just to prove me right.

An hour and a half later she's back in the recovery room, joking with nurses about her "implant." Her blood pressure is good, the bandages are in place, and soon they will release her to come home.

"So you have an immune deficiency," a nurse comments while looking at Jeanne's chart. "And the monthly infusions really help?"

"Oh, yes," Jeanne replies. "Without those infusions I don't think I'd feel half as good as I do. The infusions make all the difference."

She's lying—or maybe she's in denial. What's the difference, really? The port is in, and she's going to keep getting the infusions. A nurse brings Jeanne a turkey croissant sandwich, and Jeanne asks for mustard. "I don't think food service brought any, but I'll double-check," the nurse says as she steps toward the door.

"Oh, and I'd love a Diet Coke," Jeanne calls after her cheerfully.

Barometer Falling

It's raining, it's pouring

Nursery rhyme

It's May and the weather has turned hot and humid. I drop a handful of blueberries onto the circle of batter. Breakfast-for-dinner has always been my safety net when it's late afternoon and everyone's hungry and I haven't been to the store. This evening the sky is heavy and sultry, what Jeanne calls "close." The humidity gets between your clothes and your skin, so that coming into an air-conditioned room doesn't provide immediate relief. You have to air out; you need space, time to cool. The stovetop fan whirs, pulling up the steam and creating white noise. I flip the pancakes, then turn toward the cupboard for a platter.

She is there leaning against the counter watching me.

"Wow, Mom. You startled me."

"I'm sorry, dear. I surely didn't mean to."

So often the cough gives her away—or the light whistle in her breathing, or her shuffling steps in the house slippers—I wonder if she likes being able to sneak up on me, for once.

Jeanne gives a yank to her oxygen tubing and wheels her walker to the kitchen table. She says something I can't hear. I switch the fan off and ask her to repeat.

"Oh, I just said it looks like rain."

I turn the fan back on without replying. She sits at the kitchen table. A clap of thunder startles me and then rain pours in sheets, breaking the humidity but not enough. She speaks again. I turn the fan off. Again.

"What was that, Mom?"

"I said the rain is falling hard."

She makes conversation about nothing, as if words, any words at all, create intimacy. I long for solitude; she longs for companionship. Jeanne comments on the clouds, the rain, the drainage pattern in the backyard. "The weatherman said it would rain tonight," she says. "He sure was right. Just look at that rain come down."

I flip another pancake, then reach up and turn on the fan.

Dem Bones

Toe bone connected to the foot bone
Foot bone connected to the leg bone
Leg bone connected . . .

Negro spiritual

The summer before Jeanne moved in with us, I drove to Nebraska and helped her pack. She put her house up for sale, and the real estate agent, a church friend, told Jeanne to open windows and light candles to mask the odor of cigarettes. Jeanne was so embarrassed she couldn't look her friend in the eye. No one was supposed to know about the smoking.

Jeanne, posing as a nonsmoker, didn't own an ashtray. Instead, she smoked behind closed doors and tapped her ashes into crystal ice cream dishes. I know because as we were packing I found those small bowls, streaked with black ash, tucked in drawers and hidey-holes throughout her house.

As Zelda helps Jeanne dry off, I knock at the bathroom door.

"Fresh towels," I say. "Are you all set?"

"Oh, yes, dear. I'm decent. Clean and cozy."

I enter with the stack of towels, still warm from the dryer. Jeanne sits on her walker seat as Zelda kneels to help with a pair of socks.

"She needs her toenails clipped," I say. "Mom, did you ask Zelda about doing your toenails?" I glance at her feet. These aren't pretty feet to begin with, but today her toes are bloated and purple. They look ready to burst.

"Mom, your toes. Do they hurt?"

"Oh? I think they're always like that."

"No, Mom, they aren't. This is new."

I call Dr. Rubin's office, where the receptionist takes a message and says a nurse will phone me soon. Next I telephone Todd at work.

"Do I need to come home?"

"I'm just waiting for the nurse to call. I don't think it's an emergency."

"Well, I can bring the girls home from school. Save you the trip."

"That'll be really good. Thank you."

"Lisa?"

"Yes, what is it?"

"Thanks for taking such good care of my mom."

Six weeks after Laurie was born, Todd's parents came to visit us in Philadelphia. Jeanne knew how to calm my fussy baby, and she knew to remove the gizzard bag from the turkey *before* putting the bird in the oven. At thirty years old, I still felt like a child around her.

"Mom, I'd like to take you to meet a good friend of mine."

"Oh, I'd love to, dear."

"Her house is just two blocks over."

Jeanne gathered her purse and coat while I waited on our front stoop. When Jeanne came out of the front door, I put my head inside and called to Todd that we were leaving.

"You don't have your car keys?" my mother-in-law asked.

"I thought we'd walk," I said.

Her countenance immediately changed.

"You just had a baby, Lisa."

"I feel great. Just two blocks, and it's such a pretty day."

She didn't need to be so protective of me, and it wasn't like her—at least I didn't think it was like her. I had only been her daughter-in-law for three years.

"I'll stay here, then. I can meet your friend another time."

"But you wanted to come with me. I'm fine walking. Really."

"It's not you, Lisa. The walking . . . arthritis in my knees."

"We'll take the car, then. Not a big deal. Let me get the keys."

I have come to know the details of Jeanne's health better than she knows them herself. Her knees rarely give her problems. She has lung disease. Early signs of emphysema are shortness of breath and a cough. Lung disease develops slowly, the first symptoms coming ten, fifteen, or even twenty years before diagnosis. When I met Todd's parents, nearly twenty years ago, Jeanne had a smoker's cough so bad that people would stop and ask, *Are you sick?* She always answered no.

Chris calls me back and says something about water retention in the legs and feet signaling heart failure. My own heart speeds up. "Don't put this off," she says. Dr. Rubin has one slot open for tomorrow morning. Then Chris tells me not to worry.

I hang up the phone and double-check my calendar. I thought so. I've got a dental appointment tomorrow morning. I've already had to change it once, because two weeks ago Jeanne had a bad cough and fever that turned out to be another lung infection, but what can I do? As I dial the dentist's office to reschedule, I imagine microscopic creatures grinning as they prospect deep into my molars.

"Smoking or non?"

I shifted the phone to my other ear.

"Smoking. Double queen for two nights. First floor if at all possible. My mother-in-law can't walk far."

The night before Todd's graduation from seminary, when Laurie was just six months old, there was an awards banquet at a restaurant outside the city. After leaving the babysitter detailed instructions, we drove to the hotel to pick up Todd's parents.

"What's the room number?" Todd asked.

"One-thirty something. Umm—one-thirty-five maybe? No, thirty-three."

We asked at the desk. I'd remembered the number entirely wrong. They were on the second floor, in an even-numbered room. We took the elevator.

"This can't be right," I said.

The second floor was nonsmoking—signs on every door displayed a cigarette, circled and slashed. Even before we double-checked the number on the door, we knew by the odor which room was theirs. When my father-in-law answered the door, I saw through his breast pocket the outline of a single cigarette.

✿

After a long time in the crowded waiting room, I maneuver Jeanne's wheelchair past other patients and follow the nurse. In the exam room I set the wheelchair's brakes and take a seat.

"Lisa's worried about my piggies," she says to Dr. Rubin, lifting her feet slightly so he can remove her shoes. Gratifyingly, he is immediately concerned and leans down, palpating her feet and toes.

"Quite cold," he says. "This is poor circulation. Fluid's pooling in your feet and toes, and your heart isn't pumping as well as it used to." He scratches his head as he always does while he's considering. Sometimes he looks right at her, into her eyes, as if he can find the right treatment reflected there. Or perhaps he's trying to see whether she's telling the truth.

"The cardiologist already ruled out heart failure—are you taking the diuretic?"

"Oh, yes," she says. "Every day."

But she doesn't take it. Ever. The water pills lower her blood pressure and make her dizzy. She has to pee every fifteen minutes, reeling between bed and toilet. It's no way to live. So her ankles swell a little. Last time we were here, the doctor said no big deal. The pills are there if you need them.

I try to catch Jeanne's eye. She looks off over the doctor's shoulder.

"Umm, actually . . . she doesn't take them most days."

Jeanne shoots me a look.

"I get so dizzy," she says slowly. "I have to be in the bathroom all the time. I can't risk falling again."

"Well, for now take the diuretic. We can't have you losing toes. And elevate your feet for three hours every day. I don't mean a footstool, either. They need to be above your heart."

What kind of gymnastics is this old lady in a wheelchair going to achieve to get her feet above the level of her heart? But I know if she loses her toes she'll lose her balance. If I'm going to keep her out of a nursing home like I've promised, she has to be able to walk.

❄

Most days Todd takes the girls to school. They go with him to football games and talent shows, and all the sisters stay late when Jessica has play rehearsals—or all of them pile out to the horse barns to watch Laurie take her riding lesson. When they come home and I'm scrambling to pick up prescriptions or organize medical appointments for Jeanne, Todd coaches them through their homework. At times I feel like he's a solo parent and I'm a solo caregiver.

Todd's brothers often e-mail me and thank me for doing what they can't long distance. I send back raw news of the latest medical development or something mean she said to me or to one of the girls. They thank me, even when I gripe about Jeanne. They know how she can be. Todd remembers several times during his childhood when his mom would buy nicotine gum or a book on how to stop smoking.

"She really tried," he says. "She would tell us she had finally beaten the habit—no more cigarettes. Then smoke from under the bathroom door would give her away. It was in her clothes and on her breath. Don't know how she thought she could pass herself off as a nonsmoker."

For years Todd's mom and dad both smoked privately, each of them hiding the cigarette stash and asking for nonsmoking rooms at hotels to hold their cover. If one of the boys walked in on Jeanne smoking, it was understood that he would pretend he saw nothing, turn tail, and walk away. She expected the same from me for years.

I rant to Todd about how awful his mother is. What marriage could withstand this and remain intact? Yet ours has. If he defended his mom instead of listening to, supporting, and defending *me*, our marriage might not have survived. Todd is my retreat from his mother, but he's also the reason I have her in my life. When we married, the minister said a man must leave his parents and cleave to his wife. This worked well until our ten-year anniversary, when we bought our first home—together with Jeanne. It has been seven years.

✤

Jeanne needs blood drawn monthly so her doctor can monitor the effectiveness of her blood thinner and adjust the dosage accordingly. She takes the blood thinner to prevent stroke, since her heart doesn't pump properly. She suffers from atrial fibrillation: instead of having the steady heartbeat of a healthy person, her two upper chambers move in something closer to a quiver. This weakens the movement of the blood from the heart, so it tends to pool, making a clot more likely.

I sometimes wonder about my own heart and whether there is a symptomless defect or disease waiting in ambush. My health problems are off in the future, though no doubt being formed even now by what I eat and drink as much as by genetics. I am afraid for my future health—my future weaknesses and needs.

The medications Jeanne has taken for ten and twenty years have long-term side effects that ultimately worsen her quality of life. The steroids that ease her breathing have made her veins thin and frail—fine like threads so that they collapse when a needle is inserted. The nurses poke and probe, apologizing as veins break and blood gathers under the skin until her hands and arms are tender and bruised. The steroids also thin her skin and slow her healing. When she scrapes a knuckle, it takes weeks to heal. Jeanne's physical symptoms loop to an earlier cause, usually some medication used to address an earlier symptom, tracing back and back through the years.

Sometimes I ask myself why I hate the cigarettes so much. Even now, years after she quit, I am angry with her for smoking. I tell myself it's because all her health issues—every one—can be traced back to the cigarettes. I hated the stench and the secrets all those years. I still hate the lies. She kicked the outward habit, but the damage is done. Lung disease reaches to her very cells, and the lies go bone deep. Who am I to make this bold declaration? She who is without sin should cast the first stone.

Just out of college, I moved two hours north of my hometown to Portland to live—rent free—with a friend. A guy we knew had practically begged us to take residence in his grandmother's vacant house. My friend and I were thrilled and said yes without ever seeing the place.

As I drove into the neighborhood, my *check oil* light came on. I followed the map and pulled up next to my friend's truck in the driveway of a cute '50s rambler, situated in a low lot with trees all around. *Free rent!*

Stepping through the screen door was like entering fog. The house was stale, every surface coated with dull yellow. My friend had a bucket of Pine Sol and water and was swabbing the walls with a sponge mop. Something like dark urine dripped from the wall as she scrubbed.

"This place is disgusting," she said, grinning. "But free."

I grabbed a sponge and started scrubbing the woodwork. I wouldn't bring my boxes into this house until the stale cigarette smell was banished.

My housemate had first dibs on bedrooms, and she chose the guest room. I took the grandmother's room. I gingerly opened drawers and searched shelves until I found clean sheets. Clean? When I stripped the bed, ashes scattered to the floor. I bent down. All around the base of the bed frame stood a thick layer of cigarette ash. The slogan from my elementary school's fire safety program ran through my mind like a mantra: *Smoke in bed—wake up dead.*

I lay awake that night, repeatedly flipping my pillow to its cool side. Blanket on. Blanket off. Why hadn't we checked the condition of the house before we jumped at the free rent? Surrounded on all sides by a thin layer of ash, I finally slept.

In my dream I pounded on the crematorium door.

Instead of wiping down the bed frame after breakfast, I said I'd be back in an hour or so, and I drove my car to the nearest mechanic.

"Nearly seized up on you," he said. "You were lucky." I felt sick at the thought of living in Portland, in that house, with no car—no way of escape. Instead of returning to help clean, once my car was fixed I headed to the freeway and drove the two hours back south. I called from my parents' place with some lame excuse, and a week or so later I permanently ditched my friend with the rent-free house and all my Portland plans. I know I lied. I didn't care; I just wanted out.

✿

Jeanne describes sharp, deep pains in her chest at night in the area of the port. I am immediately on alert.

"A lot of pain, Mom?"

"Well, it keeps me awake. Only when I roll a certain way, though. Not when I'm sitting up."

"It shouldn't hurt. Not like that. I'm calling home health."

The receptionist isn't a nurse, but she sounds concerned. She will page someone—I should call back if I haven't heard within the hour.

Two hours pass, and the nurse has not returned my call about the chest pains. Should I call the doctor instead of waiting for the home health nurse? Maybe we should make a trip to the hospital. I step into Jeanne's room and hear her snoring.

I call home health again, emphasizing the unusual pain and Jeanne's discomfort. Still no contact from our nurse. By midafternoon Jeanne is up watching television, so I go to sit with her for a while—to see how much pain she had during her rest time.

"Oh, hello dear. The nurse called while you were in the restroom. She said to call her cell phone."

"Let me take a listen to the message so I can call her back."

"Tell her not to come," Jeanne says. "I haven't had that pain for at least a week."

Did she invent the pain just to gain my sympathy, my attention? Or is she so accustomed to lying that she can't tell true pain from fabricated?

"You told me you had pain last night, Mom. You couldn't sleep it was so bad."

"No, nothing like that. Don't need to bother the nurse. Nothing she can do anyway."

"But, Mom—"

"Best to call it off. I feel fine now."

I get the nurse's number off the machine, and I call her back to apologize. *No pain after all. I am so sorry.* What I am is embarrassed and angry. Did I overreact? But Jeanne said sharp chest pains, not a runny nose. This sort of thing happens more and more. Doesn't she remember the boy who cried wolf?

※

After Todd's dad died, we talked to Jeanne about moving closer to us. Over the months, we came up with a plan to buy a home together—my one restriction being that she had to have separate space, so the girls wouldn't breathe her smoke. I tromped my preschoolers through dozens of properties, but there was nothing workable on the market in our area. We decided to build, adjusting the floor plan to add a mudroom with an industrial exhaust fan as a buffer between her in-law suite and the main house where we would live.

When our new home was framed and the plumbing and wiring were under way, Jeanne came for a visit. We had appointments to select the finishing touches.

At the kitchen store a cheerful woman directed us to the part of the showroom where we were to meet with our designer. He spread out samples of countertop materials, blocks of wood to show cabinet finishes, and a glossy catalog of kitchen options. We selected cabinetry and flooring for the main kitchen and for Jeanne's kitchenette.

"Now, the hardware." The designer pulled out an open tray spread with drawer pulls.

"I need to step into the powder room before I select handles for my kitchenette," Jeanne said.

"Let's talk about the main kitchen while she's away," the designer said. "Are you sure I can't convince you to place the island closer to the counters?"

"We need the thirty-six-inch passageway on all sides," I explained. "We're planning ahead for wheelchair use someday."

"I understand. But would the wheelchair really need to fit between the dishwasher and island?"

"Maybe not. Still, I want things roomy. We've thought this through."

Jeanne returned to the showroom. From somewhere, an alarm sounded.

"Probably nothing," the designer said. "Sit tight. They'll tell us if we need to get out."

Within a few minutes, the woman who greeted us came over.

"No fire," she said to the designer. "Someone smoked in the bathroom and set it off." She turned to us, smiling. "No problem, but did either of you light up in there?"

Jeanne shook her head, "Not me."

We were the only customers in the store.

"Well, it absolutely reeks in that bathroom area now," she said. "Don't know how we'll get the smell out." Jeanne dug in her purse for a breath mint, and I didn't say a thing.

A lie by omission.

After dinner the girls clear the table so Todd and I can serve dessert. Jeanne continues eating the last of her dinner—she eats much more slowly than we do, and it's always a struggle for us to know whether to let the kids leave the table when they're finished or to stick around until their grandmother is done. We do some of each. Dessert is a good way to extend the table time, if there's not urgent homework or a school event that evening.

The girls load the dishwasher and stow leftovers. Jeanne finishes her plate as Todd scoops orange sherbet into bowls and I reach for a secret stash of chocolate Piroulines. After dessert, Todd prompts the girls to thank Mommy, and one by one, from eldest to youngest, all four say thanks and Jessica and Kayla kiss me on the cheek. From the far end of the table, Jeanne follows suit and blows me a kiss. We should serve dessert every night! I'm pleased with how something so simple slowed my family down to Jeanne's pace for a few minutes around the table. At these times, we are family.

"Teeth and pajamas," Todd tells the girls at eight-thirty.

"Will you brush my hair out, Mom?" Laurie brings me a hairbrush and I begin to work through the tangles in her long, blond hair.

"G-Mom said something today that made me mad," Laurie says.

I continue to work the brush through portions of hair.

"We were clearing the table for dessert like Dad said, and before I cleared the fruit salad I asked G-Mom if she was going to have any. She said, 'Well, I did want fruit salad, but if your mother is serving dessert that must mean I'm not allowed to keep eating dinner.' Why does she say mean stuff like that about you, Mom? It makes me so mad at her."

I want to spit. She puts my girls in the predicament of choosing between defending their mother and speaking respectfully to their grandmother. Nearly every meal, she sits at the table alone when we're done. I timed it once to see if we were out of line by eating too quickly. Todd, the girls, and I eat dinner in twenty or twenty-five minutes. She takes forty or fifty. It's not her eating that's slow. I've watched. While we're dolloping dressing on salad and cutting bites of lasagna, she stares. Mostly she stares at Laurie, who sits next to her. Todd says he wants to throw a napkin at his mother sometimes to make her stop. Laurie is able to ignore this unwanted attention much of the time, to continue laughing and talking with her sisters across the table. But sometimes she has to turn her head away from her grandmother—to hide her face.

I finish brushing out the tangles and hand Laurie the brush. I am steaming.

"Why does she do this to you girls?" Laurie of course has no answer for me. "G-Mom is not the center of this family. Why can't she just fit in?"

When we were first married, Todd used to say he didn't want to grow old—he'd rather die young and not have to deal with old age. This hurt me, because I was looking for sappy newlywed sentiments about growing old together and how the best is yet to be. Why did he want to die young when he had me?

Todd grew up with firsthand experience of family caring for family. He watched his grandparents grow old, plagued by cancer and dementia. He watched them humiliated by frailty and dependency, dying painful deaths. My mother and father moved away from their native Northwest to

Southern California before I was born, so we heard about family illnesses and deaths long distance.

I'm only now for the first time watching someone grow old and die. I finally understand my newlywed husband. I, too, want to die before I grow frail. I don't want to get old and forgetful. I don't want my children to have to live their adult lives full of tension and conflict because of me. I vow again and again that I will not live with them when I grow old.

Fourteen years ago Jeanne didn't want to walk two blocks, and now she needs a walker to get from the bed to the toilet. I worry when I leave her home alone, but I have to pick the girls up from school across town most afternoons, and I try to take a twenty-minute walk twice a week—I'd like it to be three times a week, but I usually can't manage to get away that often. I have to keep my legs, my bones, and my heart strong. I cannot let the same thing happen to me. She smoked and overate, then started taking blood pressure pills in her forties so she could keep on eating what she liked. I restrict my diet, denying myself pleasure now so that I can hold my grandkids, and so that when they run from the dinner table as soon as they finish eating, I can get up and follow right after them.

I will *not* be old and frail. There. Another lie.

Todd now embraces the prospect of growing old. He still dreads it, but he doesn't need to escape. He wonders aloud what we'll be like then, when the façade breaks down.

※

Laurie takes her shower and Todd sits down on the couch with me.

I say, "Why can't she be part of our family instead of trying to pry us apart?" Months ago I would have marched downstairs and confronted her—but that does no good. It just makes things tense and awful between us. "Todd, I wish I could divorce her. I want it to end. I want her to get so sick she will finally—"

"Sweetie, I know. But Laurie doesn't need to hear that. The girls see you struggle. It's hard for them, too, and we don't want their memories of childhood to be filled with a mommy who was angry and complained all the time." Yeah, I think. But I do complain all the time. If they saw inside me, they would see Mommy the bitch. That's who I am with Jeanne so much of the time—at least on the inside. That's the secret *I'm* hiding from *her*. And from my girls.

I express myself so freely to Todd, and he takes it. I rail against his mother, and he's rarely defensive. Never hurt. How is it *she* raised him? I have her to thank for this fine husband. I have him to thank for her presence in my life.

"When we're old ourselves," Todd says, "we'll probably be weird in our own ways. We want our girls to be able to treat us well then; we have to show them by treating my mom well now. It's for Mom, but it's also for the future. For all of us."

As I drive Jessica home from a birthday party, she asks, "Mom, what do you think I should do when I grow up? One, own a country store. Two, live in England and be an actor on *Doctor Who*. Three, be a counselor at family camp."

"Well, Jessa," I say, "How about you have a country store in England *and* be an actor for *Doctor Who* on the side *and* come back to the US in the summer to work at family camp?"

We told our kids the truth about Santa from the beginning, and when they lose a tooth they know that Mommy and Daddy are the ones to slip something special under the pillow. But I see we're not entirely truthful with them. No Santa or Tooth Fairy, but we're passing down a mythology nonetheless.

"You can do all three, Jessica. You don't have to choose."

"Mom, that's a great idea! And you can come live with me. You can run the store while I'm at my acting job."

"In England? Hmm. I might like that. Can Daddy come?"

"Of course. Just sit behind a wooden desk and if people come in the store you greet them and help them find what they need. I'll even pay you."

"Sounds good to me, Jessa."

"Oh, Mom, I wish I could just grow up and do these things now," she says.

When Jessica and I get home, Todd suggests we go to a movie while G-Mom is napping—just us and the girls. On the way there Jessica tells her sisters how she's going to do everything—England, country store, camp counselor—all of it.

"And Mommy will live in England and run my store sometimes!"

"Hey, wait a minute," Laurie protests. "Mom promised to live with *me* when she's old. She's going to build a cottage and live on a corner of my property in the country." I vaguely remember this plan.

Ashley, shocked to find that I've cheated on her, says, "No way. Mom's going to live in China with me when I'm a missionary. Dad, too."

"Glad to know I'm welcome somewhere," Todd says from the front seat. He's watching me as much as he's watching the road. "Looks like they're on to you, Lisa."

"Daddy—we just figured out that Mom promised to live with each of us!"

They're on to me all right. I didn't realize I was making promises. I pretended and went along with their fantasies, all the while thinking to myself, *I will never be a burden to my children. My children will not go through what I have these past seven years with Jeanne.*

Todd buys our tickets and holds the door as we file in. "You have a lovely family," an older woman says to me as she waits for us to pass. "Such sweet girls. Oh, they do grow up so fast, don't they?" I smile and nod as I follow my family into the cool theater lobby.

The houselights have already been dimmed. The theater is crowded and we have to sit separately, Todd and I in the center section, our four daughters all together across the aisle. In the middle of the movie I lean forward and look over, to see them as a stranger might. My eyes are accustomed to the semidarkness, and I see the girls' faces clearly. They laugh, and I want to catch a glance and share the fun, but their eyes are all on the screen. None of us knows what will come next. I take Todd's hand and turn my eyes forward.

❖

When I was a child Jessica's age, I never knew how to answer the question,

What will you be when you grow up? I would answer, "A bookworm," and slip away from the adults and their questions. When we traveled by car, I sat in the back deck of our International Harvester, facing the rear and watching the road pass behind me. I looked at where we had traveled, not where we were going.

If I live long enough, I will grow frail. No matter how well I eat or how many laps I swim each week, I will most likely need help a few decades down the road.

I've been blaming Jeanne for years. She overate, smoked, and lied. I obsess about tracing the medications and lies, joint by joint and bone by bone back in time to a first cause. I can't change the past; I cannot even truly probe and uncover it. I need a different quest.

The drive home from the movie theater is familiar. I sit in the passenger's seat beside Todd. Our girls face forward along with us, in these days of safety and seat belts and minivans with room for a large family. As we turn the last corner toward home, Jessica asks, "Can I push the remote to open the gate, Daddy?"

"Sure you can. Hurry, now."

Jessa clicks off her seat belt and comes forward to hunch between Todd and me in the space between the bucket seats. She takes the remote and presses the button. Ahead of us, the gate slides open.

A New Season

There was a crooked man
And he went a crooked mile

Nursery rhyme

It is the end of September when Dr. Rubin diagnoses the first bedsore, telling Jeanne and me that once bedsores begin, the skin keeps breaking down, and things will only get worse. Medicare will pay for the rental of a hospital bed with an alternating-pressure air mattress. He recommends a wound specialist for the bedsores, perhaps someone who can see her on a weekly basis. After writing the name of the wound care center on a slip of paper and handing it to me, Dr. Rubin leaves the room to fill out a form required by Jeanne's long-term care insurance so we can get more help at home.

As usual, Chris has a hard time accessing a vein. "Oh, I'm so sorry," she says as Jeanne's shoulders tighten. The needle is under the skin, but the veins all slip away from Chris's attempts—like she's trying to spear a noodle from a bowl of chicken soup using a dull toothpick. She pulls the needle out of Jeanne's arm and presses a cotton ball over the wound. "Let's try the back of your hand this time. This one looks pretty good," she says, tapping a thin blue vein.

"I sure wish you could just use the port to take blood," Jeanne says. Not once since she had the port installed has it been used for a blood draw.

"We don't have Huber needles," Chris explains, slipping a fresh needle under Jeanne's skin. "Oh, good, I'm in." Blood flows slowly through the tubing and drips into the sample tube.

"Chris," I say, "what would you think of Jeanne refusing a blood draw?"

"Honestly, a lot of times it's routine but not truly necessary." She turns to Jeanne. "I'd understand if you said no, Mrs. Harris." Chris seals the sample tube and removes the needle from Jeanne's hand.

"I never want to be a difficult patient," Jeanne says.

"This is the strangest thing," Chris says, shaking the test tube. "The blood is clotting right here in the tube. Let me check with Dr. Rubin before you leave."

Chris returns with instructions for Jeanne to be sure and take her Coumadin tonight. "Nothing to worry about," she says. "We'll run the prothrombin time to see if your blood really is clotting too quickly, and I'll call you tomorrow to adjust the Coumadin dosage." She hands me the completed form for long-term care, in an unsealed envelope.

When we get home and I'm alone, I unfold the form and read it. O_2 *dependency. Early decubitus ulcers. COPD—end stage. Return to independence not expected. Cognitive impairment, symptoms first appeared in past year. General prognosis poor.*

This documentation stuns me. If she is in such poor condition, why hasn't Dr. Rubin said this to Jeanne—or to me, her caregiver? Some faceless insurance adjuster is privy to more detailed information about Jeanne's health and prognosis than we are.

We could have approached the long-term care insurance company months ago and asked for a paid caregiver. Why have I tried to do so much for so long?

Before sending the form to the insurance company, I place the page on my scanner and e-mail a copy of it to Scott, to Jeff, to Todd.

Prognosis

Higher than a house, higher than a tree
Oh! Whatever can that be?

Nursery rhyme

Just a few days after the appointment with Dr. Rubin, I ask my friend Kathleen to stay with Jeanne and the girls so Todd and I can meet Jeff and his girlfriend for Tex-Mex. The headmaster from the school in Newberg called again after all these months. The position at his school is still open, and he asked Todd, "When might you be available? Can we talk about next year?"

We arrive at the restaurant first, so we order drinks and rehearse our agenda one last time. It's probably presumptuous to dare think of moving in a year or two, to assume that Jeanne may die that soon. But now that the door to a job in the Northwest has swung open again, we feel pressed to offer a more concrete answer. How long can we keep our life, our girls' lives, on hold?

Jeff arrives along with his girlfriend Pam, who serves as chaplain for a local hospice. Pam stands quiet and confident, tall and trim in a batik skirt and white T-shirt, Birkenstocks on her feet. Although we don't know it yet, Pam, too, has an agenda for the evening's conversation.

✿

A few weeks from now, we will understand better the events leading up to this conversation over chips and salsa. We will learn that when Jeff read the doctor's report aloud to Pam, he puzzled at my surprise. We already know that Jeanne is in poor health and won't live more than another year or two, he said to Pam. My shock didn't make sense to him.

After Jeff went home that night, Pam noticed the open file on her computer and sat down to examine it for herself.

The doctor's form could have been a hospice admittance record. Too many of Pam's own clients entered hospice care just days or weeks before death, not allowing them enough time to see about unfinished business, whether financial, relational, or spiritual.

I have to bring it up with Jeff's family, Pam thought. *They don't realize.*

✧

Jeff is the one to raise the topic. "Todd, if you're offered the perfect job in the part of the country where you want to live," Jeff says, "you can't turn it down. I'll take care of Mom, though I don't think I could have her living in my home like you do."

"Oh, if she's still alive in two years she will need full-time care anyway," I say. As if I know.

"What has her doctor said about prognosis?" Pam asks, sipping her beer. "In terms of decline?"

"He doesn't say," I answer. "We've tried to ask him. He smiles and says, 'Let's cross that bridge when we come to it.' Anyway, I thought hospice required a specific diagnosis—lung cancer with only a few months left to live, or something like that."

"Not necessarily," Pam says. "Jeanne has a chronic condition—the lung disease—and she will eventually die from it. The question is whether that might happen in the next six months. Not that she *will* die in the next six months, but that the doctor wouldn't be surprised if she did."

"Her doctors don't want to talk about it," I say. "Not her primary, not the immunologist, and not the pulmonologist."

"What about a second opinion?" Pam asks. "One of the doctors from our hospice covers your area—I could talk to her." While receiving hospice care, Jeanne would be at home, Pam explains. She would receive medications delivered to our doorstep. A nurse would take over the case management—all the things I've been doing myself. Jeanne could relax and enjoy the rest of her life as much as possible.

It feels like Pam is trying to push Jeanne into a coffin. At the same time,

I'm glad we're talking. How often have I wished it could be the end? Would it be different if I were the daughter and not the daughter-in-law?

"It has to be one of you guys who talks to Jeanne about this," I say, looking from Todd to Jeff. "When the time comes, I mean." It feels like we're all playing roles—pretending that Jeanne is near her deathbed, rehearsing for an event that's probably still years away.

None of us can see the future, that just one week from now Jeanne will make her decision, led to that point not by sons or a daughter-in-law but by an intractable infection.

Seek Shelter

Ladybird, ladybird, fly away home!

Nursery rhyme

Around dinnertime on March 28, 2000, the skies over Fort Worth turned an ominous green. Warning sirens screamed, and at 6:20 p.m. the first tornado slammed into downtown. Another followed. Both were categorized as strong F2 or low-end F3: they spun at 150 to 200 miles per hour and were capable of tearing roofs off frame houses, demolishing weak buildings, and flattening manufactured homes or trailers. In a tornado this strong, large trees are snapped or uprooted; semis and boxcars are tossed on their sides; cars are swept off highways.

In Reata, the restaurant on the thirty-seventh floor of the Bank One Tower, people dashed into the stairwell for shelter while powerful winds sent furniture flying and blew apart interior walls.

The tornadoes killed four people and injured more than one hundred.

Large sections of downtown were closed off for weeks; in the buildings struck by one tornado or the other, broken glass hung loosely and then plummeted in sheets, collapsing against the ground. Six large commercial buildings downtown were badly damaged. Experts estimated the overall damage to Fort Worth at more than $450 million. In the months following the tornadoes, some buildings, such as the Calvary Cathedral, were razed, while others, such as the Cash America Building, were rebuilt.

When we moved to Texas in 2003, two condemned towers still stood vacant against the Fort Worth skyline. The once shimmering, thirty-seven-story Bank One skyscraper lost 80 percent of its windows in the storm. They were replaced or covered over with plywood for safety, so that locals called it Plank One Tower. Asbestos insulation prevented safe demolition, and the lack of a buyer willing to renovate meant that the city could neither tear down nor rebuild.

Cash America, one of the buildings hit hardest by the tornado, housed the FBI. The tornado spun their files out into the streets like a millionaire tossing his money to the crowds. FBI agents scrambled to gather the scattered documents, their secrets thrown to the winds.

❖

Just four days after our dinner date with Jeff and Pam, Jeanne wakes with her left foot swollen, red, and tender to the touch. Jeanne and I both fear a blood clot that may break loose and travel to her heart or lungs. I help Jeanne into the wheelchair and out to the car, and as we drive out of the neighborhood I call Dr. Rubin's office on my cell phone and ask for Chris.

"I'm bringing Jeanne to your office right now," I explain, cataloging the symptoms. "I'm hoping Dr. Rubin can check it and tell us whether to head on to the emergency room."

"Take her straight to the hospital," Chris says in a level voice. "We don't have a Doppler here. Call me later to tell me what happens, will you?"

I relay the news to Jeanne and she purses her lips.

Twice this past summer her oxygen saturation dropped below 70 percent from her personal norm of 95 percent. I honored her wishes. No trip to the ER. Instead, I cranked the oxygen flow as high as it would go, and both times her levels rose. A month later when I told Dr. Fletcher about the incident, he said she really should have gone to the hospital. With levels that low, they might need to intubate. Jeanne looked him in the eye and said she did *not* want to be intubated under any circumstances, and that when the time came she wanted to die at home. He nodded and told me I had done all that an ER nurse would do, short of intubation. "Let's be optimistic, Mrs. Harris, and say we'll see you in six months."

This time when we arrive at the hospital, Jeanne is immediately wheeled straight through triage and deep into the ER for an examination of the painful foot. We are at the hospital four hours: Doppler, EKG, prothrombin time, CBC. No blood clot. Still, the pain and tenderness and swelling persist. When the nurse comes to remove the EKG wires and get Jeanne ready for discharge, she notices something new.

"Have you seen this?" she asks. The area of Jeanne's chest where the port lies under the skin is as red and swollen as her foot. A chill spreads through my gut.

"It is kind of sore," Jeanne says.

But the ER doctor does not seem particularly concerned about the area of infection around the port. Nor about her foot, which is still the source of the most pain.

"Might be cellulitis in the foot," he says. "And see your doctor this week about the port."

The nurse brings Jeanne a prescription for an antibiotic, and we leave the hospital.

When we arrive back home, Jeanne is exhausted. She goes right to bed.

In today's mail is a thick envelope from the long-term care insurance company. I tear it open and read the cover letter twice to make sure I understand correctly. They recommend ten hours a day, seven days a week of custodial care—someone to help with meals, dressing, showers, everything. This is the maximum benefit, the letter warns, and the policy will cover only six years at this rate. Six years—Jeanne will not live six more years.

After calling to update Chris at Dr. Rubin's office, I phone the immunologist to tell him about the infected port.

"The doctor is out of town for three weeks," his receptionist says. "One of the nurses will have to see you." I open my calendar and write the appointment time for the next day.

✲

Living in North Texas means that we have tornado scares a few times each year. "Seek shelter immediately," the electronic voice on the weather radio will say, and we do. The girls and I take shelter, that is. Not Todd. He goes outside, looks into the wind, and comes back to turn on the news.

Todd grew up in Indiana—storm country—and he knows the difference between a watch and a warning. I grew up in Southern California, and when we moved to Texas it took me month after nervous month to learn that tornado *watch* means the weather pattern *could* produce a tornado, while tornado *warning* means that a rotation has been spotted on or near the ground. When our county is under a tornado warning, the funnel rotation may be miles off and headed away from us. Still the sirens wail. Todd watches the icons on the weatherman's map or listens for the geographical position of the rotation before he decides whether or not to join us in the closet.

To take shelter or not when the warning is given? Once, the sirens blared and I looked out to see sun and only a few light raindrops. The sirens said yes, but there were no signs of an impending vortex. I called the girls to come, and we hid in the closet while the sun shone, until the sirens faded to silence.

Jeanne wakes the next morning with blood and pus on her gown. Over the port are two holes—dammit, what is going on? Vampire bite, I joke, but I'm repulsed and worried. This can't be good, can't even be okay. I cover the port site with gauze. The visiting nurse, who checks on Jeanne twice a week, calls to say she is in the area, just down the block, is it okay if she stops by?

When Diane arrives she looks at Jeanne's swollen foot and leg with concern. "I've seen this before," she says. "Your heart isn't pumping that fluid back out of the leg. See here?" She points to what look like blisters up and down Jeanne's shins. "These are stasis ulcers. They can get infected and become really painful."

"What are they from?"

"Your circulation isn't moving the fluid. It's nothing we can fix."

Jeanne leans on her walker and steps gingerly to the bathroom, cringing with each step on the sore foot. She shuts the bathroom door behind her.

"Diane, I know you're not a doctor and I won't take anything you say as gospel," I say in a low voice. "Will this get better? I mean, are we looking at the end of life here?"

Diane stops poking at her laptop and looks straight at me. "Her body is shutting down, Lisa. None of this will get better."

"So, off the record, do you think she'll live another year?"

"I can't imagine a year. This is just what I've seen from doing home health, but . . . maybe months."

"Do you think she would be a candidate for hospice?"

"I wish she could be, Lisa. But they won't take her if she insists on continuing with the infusions and all the treatments. It might be—"

Jeanne returns from the bathroom.

"You know, Mrs. Harris, if I were you I would have them take that port out. Give up those infusions—they aren't doing you any good, are they?"

I freeze. I can't look at Jeanne, though I nod in agreement with Diane.

"You're right," Jeanne says. "They don't help."

❈

The vampire bite has merged into a quarter-sized hole by the time the immunologist's nurse checks on it in the afternoon. He peels back the gauze and in the open hole I see the rounded corner of the port, metallic purple under the ooze of blood and fluid.

"I've seen worse," the nurse says. He peels a sterile wrapper off a huge Q-tip and swabs fluid from the port site while Jeanne cringes. He inserts the sample into a tube to be sent to the lab.

"Will they need to remove the port?" I ask.

"I think so," he says. "With the doctor out of town, I'm not sure what to do. I need someone else to look at it. Can you come back tomorrow? Without a doctor here, our physician's assistant is the only one who can schedule a surgery."

From home I call Dr. Rubin's office and ask for Chris.

"Her port site looks awful and the immunologist is out of town," I explain. "There's no solution in sight yet."

"I'm so sorry," Chris says.

"What I called to ask you is whether Dr. Rubin—what his feelings are about hospice and in what circumstances he would refer a patient. We're starting to think Jeanne might be a candidate."

"Oh, hospice is wonderful," Chris says warmly. "I can't say enough good things about hospice. There are several of our patients I would love to see receiving hospice care, and Eugenia is at the top of my list."

What? Chris looks at Jeanne and thinks *She should be under hospice care* and no one tells me?

"Dr. Rubin—he's old school, and the concept goes against his training," Chris continues. "We're working on him. He still has the feeling that hospice hastens death, but he's coming around."

"Do you think he would give her a referral?"

"You don't need that," Chris says. "If she's hospice appropriate, a doctor or nurse from hospice will admit her. When that happens Dr. Rubin will fax his agreement to hospice so he can continue to follow her case."

"Really? We can seek hospice care without a doctor sending us there? No blood gas or other tests?"

"Oh, yes," says Chris. "In fact she'll get a better level of health care than she's getting now. A hospice doctor will see her in the home, manage her care there, and let Dr. Rubin know what's going on. She won't have to go to the hospital, the ER, or do anything else she doesn't want to do."

Chris is so enthusiastic, as if we're sending Jeanne on a free cruise.

I finally realize that the experts, all these specialists, the ones who are supposed to be the educators of their patients, have been looking at Jeanne and seeing a dying woman. But they kept sending us all over Fort Worth on wild goose chases, despite the mass of physical ailments signaling that Jeanne is at the end of her life. Why the hell didn't anyone speak up?

❖

Until the 1940s there were no weather warnings specifically for tornadoes, no sirens or weather watch alerts. The weather bureau had no way to forecast these acts of God. When the day grew dark and the winds blew, folks knew to keep an eye out for the signs: sickly green skies under swirling clouds, falling hail, the sound of a rushing waterfall turning to a roar. You had to watch out for your elderly neighbor in those days—maybe she was busy with canning in the kitchen and hadn't looked out the window. Deaf from age, she might not have heard the storm. You had to warn her, to help her, to run and take her hand.

You can stock your storm cellar ahead of time, place a Bible and a kerosene lamp on the table to get through the darkness. But these well-laid plans do no good unless you actually go to the safe room, unless you get there before the tornado overtakes you. When a tornado comes your way, roiling and riotous, all you can do is hunker down until it's over.

❧

The port site looks a bit better when we return the next day for a "second opinion" at the doctorless office. Jeanne still has a hole in her chest, oozing a little but not as angry and red. The foot, though—Jeanne can hardly bear weight on it today. She has to take a Darvocet, then two, just to stand and pivot from the bed to the wheelchair. I worry helping her into the car that she will fall. Three days in a row of medical excursions and no sign of relief ahead. Can't someone at least prescribe a stronger painkiller?

The physician's assistant looks at the port site, but the leg seems to be her greater concern. The antibiotic from the emergency room has made no visible difference, and she says she suspects that the swollen foot and leg are symptoms of a circulation problem and not an infection at all. Just like Diane said yesterday.

"I wonder," I say quietly, testing, "if her body is just wearing out. Poor circulation—is that the heart giving up?"

"Yes," says the assistant. "I'm sure you're right." She directs the nurse to bring her a clean lancet and gauze. She lances one of the stasis ulcers, which Jeanne doesn't feel, and it oozes fluid, releasing pressure. The nurse holds his fingers against Jeanne's leg and looks at his watch, checking the pulse. When the assistant and nurse make eye contact, the nurse shakes his head.

"The circulation is poor in your leg, Mrs. Harris," the assistant says. "This light wrap will compress the fluid, forcing it up and hopefully relieving some pain." She explains to me that the fluid may only go as high as the bandage and then pool in her upper leg. "If it does that, don't worry, because there's nothing more you can do," she says. "Call us if her toes turn black."

Jeanne flexes her knee to test the feel of the wrapped leg and foot.

"Now, let's get a CBC. Is that okay with you, Mrs. Harris?"

"Only if you give me someone who can get in and get out quickly and not poke and poke."

"Mom," I say. "You can say no." So many blood tests over the months, and the results nearly always come back inconclusive except for an elevated white blood count from whatever infection is active in her body at the time. We wait for Jeanne's reply.

"I'll let them take the blood," she says.

A nurse sticks a needle just under the skin on the back of Jeanne's hand and probes for a full five minutes, Jeanne drawing in her breath through clenched teeth the whole time. I turn my head away. Then I hear the rustle of the nurse gathering plastic and paper wrappers. Jeanne's hand is bruised and blackened and more pooled blood puffs up under her skin. The nurse applies pressure.

"I got in a couple of times, and the veins blew," she explains to her colleague. "Can you try?"

I step around to the front of the wheelchair and kneel before Jeanne, face to face with her. "Mom, you can say no. Do you want to tell them not to do it?" The nurses both wait for her answer—maybe they won't have to pierce and jab this woman again.

"What is the blood work for?" I ask the nurses.

They do not know.

"Mom, let's just go home."

"I want the blood drawn." Jeanne holds out her other arm.

I can't watch. I leave the room to stand in the hallway. My face to the wall, I wipe away tears. I am starting to see through new eyes: an old lady dying, her body withdrawing, tucking like a turtle into its shell. And Jeanne is not ready to turn away the needles, to stop treatment and consider hospice. We must keep doing the next thing, the next thing, even when we don't know why or whether it will help. No one says, *That's enough.* Not even me.

❖

One stormy April afternoon, trackers recorded a rotation southwest of the school my children attend. Tornado sirens screamed. No one at school thought to set off the disaster alarm sequence. Laurie remembers that her class filed out into the first-floor hallway and crouched against the wall with heads tucked and hands clasped behind necks to protect themselves in case of flying glass. Jessica, on the other end of the building, recalls how her teacher calmed frightened students with an impromptu storytelling session. "Tuck your heads like little snails and listen, children. When I was a child in West Texas, oh, we had storms. This one right now—it's nothing compared to West Texas. Why, one time . . ."

Ashley, too, recalls the disruption in the hall that day. Outside her second-floor classroom, students rushed back and forth, teachers calling out instructions. As hail pattered on the windows and lightning flashed, Ashley's class went right on singing their song about the history of the Middle Ages, not hearing sirens outside and only mildly irritated by the chaos in the hallway.

"Shut that door, please," the teacher said to Ashley. "Too much noise."

Before Ashley shut the door, she peeked out into the hall.

"Umm, I think there's a tornado drill," she said to her teacher.

"No tornado drill scheduled," the teacher said. "Go back to your desk please, Ashley."

The tornado that fingered earth near my kids' school retracted into the swirling storm seconds after the sirens went off. Ashley's teacher closed her book and told the class to take out their math assignments as the rest of the students in the school reluctantly filed back to their classrooms, grabbing quick slurps at the water fountain. What if the tornado had touched down and churned a path right into the school building? No one warned Ashley's class to take shelter. The thought haunts me.

❖

The next morning I wait until after Todd and the girls leave for school before I check on Jeanne. I'm anxious over what new ailments may have developed overnight. She lies on her back in bed, the walker standing by her night table. She moves her hand to wipe her cheek, but she doesn't greet me, doesn't turn her head. Jeanne stares at the ceiling.

"Morning, Mom. I need to check your toes and change the bandage on your port."

Her toes are not black. The port site has oozed all the way through both layers of gauze. I put on a fresh dressing and tape it lightly in place. Jeanne turns her eyes to me.

"I feel so guilty," she says slowly. "I know you're sick of taking care of me." She looks back to the ceiling. "All I feel is guilt."

That's what she thought it meant when I left the room as they were trying to draw blood yesterday—that I was sick of taking care of her! I don't know how to respond. Yes, I am sick of the daily doctor appointments and useless procedures. I don't want her to hurt and keep hurting.

"Mom, please look at me." I sit beside her on the bed. "When I saw them digging for your blood sample yesterday, I couldn't even watch. I didn't want you to hurt for something that does no good." I begin to cry. "I wanted to protect you."

Jeanne reaches out to take my hand.

"None of it is helping you, Mom," and before I can think through whether I should or not, I say it all: "I talked to Chris yesterday and she told me she wished you'd consider hospice. Is it time, Mom? The bedsores have started. The stasis ulcers just get worse. Now this fluid in your leg— it's a circulatory problem. We can't fix any of it. I wasn't even going to be the one to bring it up with you, but here we are. Oh, Mom, are you ready to talk about hospice?"

She doesn't have to pause even a moment.

"You know I'm ready, Lisa. Maybe it's time. But how do we do it? Yes, I'm ready."

We hold hands; we talk and cry. I feel such love for Jeanne right now. Have I really resented caring for her? It seems like such a short time that she has needed me.

"Oh, Lisa, I just know I don't want to be poked anymore. I don't want them to take any more blood."

The day has come.

Jeanne begins to talk about her will, about cremation and burial.

"Aren't we putting the cart before the horse?" I ask. "We need the hospice admission first, don't we?"

"I want Virginia," Jeanne says. "Will you call her? I have to be sure I'm making the right decision." She also asks me to call her minister, Betsy.

"Lisa, see if they can come today. If I'm going to decide, I don't want to wait any longer." She wants a blessing.

Betsy and Virginia come in the afternoon. They are not shocked or appalled. Betsy nods and says, "Jeanne, this is wise."

Virginia, who worked many years as a nurse herself, says, "Jeanne, you are not ever going to get better."

Betsy prays and there are more tears. And peace. We don't need to run to the doctor's office or the emergency room ever again. No more needles, and soon no more pain.

❈

Chris tells me that when she brings Dr. Rubin the hospice forms and tells him Jeanne has decided to receive comfort care only, he lowers his head and slowly nods. "Yes. It's time," he says.

The hospice nurses say that Jeanne probably was hospice admissible six or nine months ago. We waited too long. Even while I'm relieved that we're at the end, I'm angry with the doctors who kept ordering blood draws and treatments that stole Jeanne's time and comfort. Had we known Jeanne was eligible, she might have had a few stable months with comfort care in the home.

❈

Sometimes the storm is louder than the sirens, and the electricity goes out—the tornado will soon touch down. Your elderly neighbor is limping, and you know she cannot outrun the storm. Take her hand. Lead her to the safe room and tell her it's time to rest. Tuck a quilt around her and hold her hand while overhead the clouds churn, the sky goes greenish gray, the wind bears down like a freight train.

Thirty-One Days

As I was going along, along
A-singing a comical song, song, song
The lane that I went was so long, long, long
And the song that I sang was so long, long, long
And so I went singing along

Nursery rhyme

Day 1

On a pain scale of 1 to 10, Jeanne puts the pain in her infected foot at a 9. The hospice nurse starts her on liquid morphine, one of the medications provided in the "comfort pack" we receive when Jeanne signs the hospice paperwork. It'll take a few doses before she notices a difference, most likely. We can dose every hour. Despite the continuing pain, I see a difference in Jeanne, an ease. She will die at home, and the hospice workers will provide all care for Jeanne here at the house.

"Once we have the pain under control, we can keep you comfortable right to the end," the hospice doctor promises Jeanne. "You must be very careful to always dose her on time," the doctor turns to me. "It's easier to control the pain than to eliminate it once it starts up again. Medicate ahead of the pain. If you don't and the pain returns, she could have a pain crisis—severe pain, uncontrollable or very hard to bring back under control."

By tomorrow we'll have extended-release tablets for morphine dosage, and the liquid morphine will be only for breakthrough pain. The doctor instructs me on each medication—lorazepam, for anxiety, can be dissolved in water when Jeanne has trouble swallowing, senna for constipation that comes with the morphine. Do not dissolve the twelve-hour morphine tablets in water. Don't let her crush them between her teeth, don't break them in half if we miss a dose: breaking, crushing, or dissolving the pill could mean a lethal dose—twelve hours of morphine all at once may kill her.

Scott and Michelle will fly with the kids in a few days to spend a week or so, to say good-bye. Jeff, now living an hour north of Fort Worth, will come on Tuesdays and Thursdays and on the weekends.

They say it will take only a week or two before the infection at her port site spreads to every system: sepsis, then death. The oral antibiotics have already failed. She could go to the hospital for intravenous treatment, but that would mean more needles, blood pressure cuffs, all that Jeanne wants to be done with. The infections are eventually going to win. At least this time it's not pneumonia. Medications will keep her comfortable, and death from sepsis will be much easier for her than end-stage emphysema. Two weeks, maybe three. I thought we would be instructed to discontinue all medications, but the hospice doctor told me how to little by little eliminate the bigger pills as she has a harder time swallowing. "Let nature take its course" is a complex principle. We pushed nature off course a long time ago, with procedures and medications that seemed, at the time, to help more than they harmed.

When she's not sleeping, Jeanne's eyes are glassy and her pupils contract to tiny dots.

Day 2

The pain is better. Still there, but she puts it at a 5 now. Jeanne is so drugged. She complains that her mouth is dry.

"I need to use that mouth spray that moisturizes," she says.

I can't think what she means. Saline spray? "Is your *nose* dry, Mom?" I ask.

"No, my mouth. I need the mouth spray."

I reach for the nasal saline spray we keep under the sink, and I hand it to her. She squirts saline in her mouth a few times and sucks on the nozzle.

Day 3

Jeanne is finally pain free. She's groggy and weak from the morphine. When I take her to the bathroom, she cannot stand from the wheelchair to sit on the toilet. I move the hospice's portable commode to her bedside.

The hospice nurse says that if Jeanne doesn't eat much she won't need the bathroom very often. When she is too weak to get up to pee we can request a catheter.

In the evening I make eggs for a late dinner. Jeanne isn't hungry so she stays in bed while the rest of us eat in the kitchen.

As soon as we say grace, Ashley tears into her cinnamon toast. I joke with her not to eat like a hungry cave man devouring his prey. Ashley laughs and we all laugh, and we are so relaxed around the table. This is new. No pressure for bad manners from G-Mom. No deep sighs because I'm serving breakfast for dinner again. Soon, this is what life will be like for us. Just Todd and the girls and me, every meal.

Yet even as I feel butterflies of excitement for what is ahead, grief presses at the back of my eyes. For years and years I have wished and waited for her to die and I *have* loved her and served her and taken care of her—even when I hated it—and here we are at the end. I wanted the end to come, but did I really believe it ever would? Now that her death is near, I find that I am not in a hurry.

Day 5

I wake at 4:00 a.m. and lie in bed with my eyes wide in the dark. Why am I awake? I forgot Jeanne's morphine pill last night. She's downstairs in a silent pain crisis, while the caregiver, hired with long-term care insurance funds, sleeps on in the next room. I fly downstairs to Jeanne's room, tripping over the oxygen tubing in the dark hallway. She sits awake with the head of her bed raised and the bedside lamp turned on.

"Jeanne, you're up. How do you feel?" My voice shakes.

"Fine, dear," she says. "I think I'll go to the bathroom."

The caregiver, sleeping on a mattress in Jeanne's sitting room, hears us through the baby monitor and comes into the room. She helps Jeanne up to use the bedside commode.

I also forgot Jeanne's other night meds, her heart pills and prednisone and blood thinner. I could give her the blood thinner off schedule but not the heart pill. What if I skip the other pills altogether? Will I be killing her? It's too soon to start eliminating pills—and for the wrong reason. She can still swallow. I'm just a lousy, forgetful caregiver.

When Jeanne returns from the bathroom I hand her the morphine tablet. She smiles. "Thank you, dear. Now I think I'll go back to sleep." She has no idea. And no pain.

I say quietly to the caregiver, "I forgot to dose her meds last night. I need you to help me." She nods and sets the alarm on her wristwatch.

I leave Jeanne's room and feel around the darkened hallway to check the oxygen concentrator. When I tripped, I pulled the tubing off. In the dark I feel for the connection and push it on. Something doesn't feel as it should be, so I turn on the light. I've pushed the tubing onto the humidifier bottle, not the oxygen supply. I fasten the tubing correctly and turn out the hall light.

I'm going to make mistakes as this goes on and I am shorter of sleep and more emotional. She is dying, but I don't want to kill her.

Day 6

Jeanne is different this morning, as she has been every morning. She will start a sentence and not finish. She asks who is in the room with us, as if she's blind. Todd is with her now, giving her ice chips. Probably someone fed her ice chips when she was in the hospital after giving birth to him.

Day 7

I am in the kitchen when I hear the caregiver say to one of the girls, "Where's Mommy? Get Mommy!" I dash back to Jeanne's bedroom. "More changes," the caregiver says in a low voice. "She's very confused and doesn't want to take her medication." Jeanne stares at the small handful of pills in her own hand.

"What time is it?"

"It's six in the evening, Mom. You need the morphine—the gray pill."

"I don't understand. These are my bedtime pills. Why are you trying to make me take them now? It's light outside."

I cajole back and forth with her, trying to explain. "Everything's on a twelve-hour schedule now, Mom, because of the extended-release morphine." She keeps saying she doesn't understand, as she holds the pills in the palm of her hand and watches me with hooded eyes. I try to keep calm so she won't be alarmed.

"Mom, I need you to take these pills now. We don't want the pain to come back."

Finally she consents. Now Jeanne wants to stand up, to use the bedside commode. She has wet herself, right through her panties and incontinence pad. We change her, pull off the wet stuff and sponge her clean. Then the caregiver holds Jeanne's nightgown up out of the way while I pull up her panties and make sure the fresh pad is in correct position. Jeanne stands and pivots from the commode to the side of the bed and sits. She says, "I think I'll just stand up again and have some . . . have some . . . ice cream right here on the side of my bed. But first I want to stand up. I need to be there so I can . . . so I don't . . . so that . . ."

Then Jeanne laughs, "Oh, my. I can't think straight."

Day 10

I sit with Jeanne late into the evening. She's a morphine insomniac. Just lying there, eyes open and glazed, but not sleeping. The hospice handbook says that music may soothe the dying patient, so I've brought down a CD player and put on orchestral music. She finally starts to drift off, but it seems that everything rouses her—when the music changes from strings to horns, when I close my book, when I sniff. When she finally sleeps, her feet twitch violently, and especially the swollen one. Then with a more pronounced twitching, almost kicking, she moans, "Ow, oh, ow," and wakes.

"Are you in pain, Mom?"

"No, I don't think so."

"Your foot is twitching; does it hurt?"

"It's a muscle spasm but not the kind of spasm that hurts."

Ashley comes into the room in her pajamas and sits at Jeanne's bedside. She holds her grandmother's hand.

"Ashley, is that what Little Red said?"

Sweet Ashley looks at me with a raised eyebrow, then she smiles at Jeanne and says, "Mmmm-hmm." When Jeanne is finally deeply asleep, Ashley sits on my lap—such a big girl now, at eleven—and cries into my shoulder.

Day 12

Jeanne is now too weak to safely use the bedside commode, so the hospice nurse inserts a urinary catheter. A bag of urine hangs on the side of the bed. The catheter tube will likely introduce bacteria and cause further infection, the nurse tells me quietly. "It can be a very good step," she says. "Helps things along."

I sit with Jeanne through the afternoon, writing while she dozes. She feels woozy and doesn't want to be alone. As we follow the orders from hospice to medicate ahead of the pain, I can't help wondering if what we're really doing is drugging her to death.

Day 13

Jeanne says, "Tell me this, Lisa. Why am I still here?"

"What do you mean, Mom?"

"How do they know I'm dying?"

I explain about sepsis, infection, it takes time, we don't know when, even the doctors don't know, etc., but she'll be comfortable and we'll be with her.

"Are you changing your mind, Mom? Having second thoughts about hospice?"

"No, dear. I just wonder what I'm doing wrong that it's taking so long."

Day 14

At 5:00 a.m. Jeanne needs to poop. We don't have a bedpan, and she's too weak to get out of bed. Todd drives to the twenty-four-hour Walgreens.

No bedpans. I call hospice and am told a nurse will come on duty at 8:00, and they'll see if she can bring us a bedpan. I'm tired of being courteous, of being the friendly partner with the hospice staff. I raise my voice; I insist. She's lying in bed too weak to get up to use the toilet and now she's supposed to hold her bowels for two hours? We need a bedpan *now*.

Within twenty minutes a nurse is at the door with a bedpan. She coats it with cornstarch before shoving it between Jeanne's bottom and the sheet. We raise the head of the bed and Jeanne strains for forty-five minutes before she gives up. Eventually the urge passes and Jeanne goes back to sleep.

A few hours later Jeanne opens her eyes and says, "Fruit and meat. Meat and fruit. Those are my favorite foods. Frequently when new people are here they will ask me, 'what's your favorite food?' I was just thinking, meat and fruit."

Day 17

Scott and Michelle and their kids arrive from France. They will need to sleep in Jeanne's sitting room, so we move the caregiver's mattress into Jeanne's large, carpeted bathroom, which is only used now to empty the catheter bag.

As Jeanne sleeps the caregiver whispers to me, "She's doing this so beautifully. Most people don't. Even strong Christians. You would be surprised."

The catheter bag today is full of blood.

Day 18

Jeanne's bloody urine indicates that she has a severe urinary tract and bladder infection. Lifting the catheter bag for a better look, the nurse says she sees chunks of bladder wall matter along with the blood. It's nearly impossible to believe that this is not cause for alarm, that we're not rushing to the hospital for another emergency room fix. Jeanne can't feel a thing because of the blessed morphine. With the way the urine looks, the nurse says infection will go quickly to other organs—if the kidneys become infected then urine output will slow or stop, or infection may spread to Jeanne's stomach then heart; we should expect sepsis very soon. She'll spike a fever and then lose consciousness.

When I walk the nurse to the door, she tells me that just before coming here she was at a patient briefing meeting. When she gave her update on Jeanne, the attending doctor was amazed that Jeanne is still with us.

"No one can predict these things," the nurse says, "but I wouldn't be surprised if she's unresponsive the next time I visit."

I can't believe Jeanne will ever die. I keep thinking maybe if we quit giving her morphine she would just get up and walk to the bathroom by herself, eat a nice dinner, phone a friend. Then I look at that catheter bag full of chunks and blood. I think of the hospice nurse tenderly changing the dressing over Jeanne's bedsores. I remember the last blood draw, how much trouble the nurses had finding a vein. When they took her blood pressure she grimaced because it was so painful. It's not just the morphine doing this. Her body is all used up.

Day 20

I'm either with her in that room or else seeing about feeding family, feeding guests, putting away food brought in by church folks, writing thank-you notes. One of the moms from school brings a Thanksgiving dinner, though it's the middle of October. I should be moved by this sweet gesture, but I'm not. Every minute of my life, every hour of the day is about Jeanne. Ashley needs to see the dentist. The girls all need doctor appointments and booster shots. My house is a wreck. I am tired of waiting for her to die before we can carry on living. Am I heartless if I choose not to stay in that room while she dies? Life is going on and I'm falling behind.

Day 24

Jeanne is still eating small amounts—ice cream and dark meat turkey are her only requests. She will occasionally ask for a Diet Coke but take only a sip before dozing off.

Late in the afternoon, Jeanne needs to poop again. Scott and Todd lift her to the commode, and she's so weak she cannot sit up straight. She strains but nothing happens. She's still on the commode, leaning and pushing, when I bring her night meds and a glass of water. She sips and dribbles and shifts the pills in her mouth, but can't seem to swallow. I wait and watch and then with a jolt I remember the extended-release morphine and how I am *not* supposed to dissolve it in water.

"Jeanne, give me the pills. Spit them into my hand." I reach into Jeanne's mouth with my finger to sweep out the pills. Sure enough, here is the pocked morphine.

Michelle keeps Jeanne company and watches to make sure she doesn't lose her balance and fall from the commode, while I go out to the front of the house to call hospice and leave a message for the on-call nurse. When I return to the bedroom and ask Jeanne if she's having any luck, she answers in total nonsense.

"We should get her back in bed right now," I say.

"Yes," Michelle says. How much morphine has Jeanne sucked in at one dose? Scott lifts her back into bed. When the nurse arrives, she asks if Jeanne has been eating. Yes, she had turkey and salad for lunch, we say.

The nurse winks at me as she says to Jeanne, "So you had turkey for lunch and tonight you can't swallow your pills? Maybe we should wrap them in turkey."

She asks for a dish of ice cream and perches the pocked morphine tablet on top of a spoonful. "These can be administered rectally, too," she comments. Michelle and I share a glance.

"She's doing fine," the nurse says. "Give her the pills with ice cream and she'll be able to swallow them."

I'm relieved that Jeanne has taken the morphine, but I'm also disappointed that it is not yet time for continuous care, for hospice to take over the dosing. I walk the nurse to the door, and at the porch she turns to me.

"When you're caregiving out of love you can't make a mistake," she says. I nod numbly, say thank you, and close the door.

What the hell does that mean? As long as I love Jeanne I should feel free to give her a massive dose of morphine? I must have misunderstood.

Day 28

Today Jeanne is confused and restless. She hears Todd call to the girls from the other part of the house, and she calls back, "I'm coming" and tries to climb over the bedrails. When the girls are in the room, Jeanne becomes agitated. I tell them to stay out. Even with ice cream, Jeanne can't swallow. A striped capsule of heart medication sticks on the back of her tongue and I imagine her drawing in one quick breath and sucking it into the wrong tube. She manages to swallow the heart medication, but I go through her pills and pull out anything bigger than the morphine tablets.

Day 29

I don't even try the ice cream. I dissolve lorazepam in a few drops of water and mix it with pudding.

"Open your mouth, Jeanne. Mmmm, good pudding, just a taste to help get your medicine down." I'm baby talking to my mother-in-law. Jeanne seems thick and stiff. She opens her mouth, but when I place the spoon of pudding against her tongue she doesn't close her mouth, doesn't seem to remember how to eat from a spoon. I scrape the spoon against her teeth to drop the pudding into her mouth. It sits on her tongue. She does not swallow. I don't dare risk the morphine tablet, so I give her drops of liquid morphine, hoping they will absorb through her cheeks if she doesn't swallow, hoping she won't choke on the pudding and morphine. I call hospice and receive instructions to continue dosing liquid morphine every couple of hours until a nurse can come and evaluate the situation.

When the nurse arrives several hours later, Jeanne is in a deep sleep and can't be roused.

"It's time for continuous care," the nurse says. I begin to cry for relief.

The nurse points out light mottling on Jeanne's legs due to decreasing circulation.

"This is a sign we're nearing the end," she says. "Any time now, really."

With the way this has gone so far, we've still got days and days.

Day 30

When I wake and go in to check on Jeanne, the continuous care nurse is sleeping, too, there in the chair beside Jeanne's bed. Jeanne looks peaceful but I am disconcerted—should this nurse be sleeping? The day passes, a Saturday, with no drama, no big changes, only more of a rattle in her breathing.

Day 31

Sunday morning. I have just started my coffee brewing when the nurse comes out to the kitchen, seeming shaken, to tell me. I call upstairs to Todd, but I am the first one to Jeanne's side.

Her eyes are closed. I touch her cool arm; I imagine the rise and fall of her chest, right where the blood and pus have been draining, where we've bandaged so carefully so she won't have any more pain.

Her death certificate will say myocardial infarction, caused by coronary artery disease exacerbated by lung disease—Dr. Rubin will sign the death certificate having never seen the body.

I am neither nurse nor daughter, but I set down this history to record my own witness: the port is what killed her.

Her body lies still and naked. The nurse pulls on surgical gloves; I do not. I reach my arms around Jeanne and draw her onto her side. I hold her as the nurse removes the disposable pad and changes the sheet. I gently touch a fresh abrasion on Jeanne's arm; it does not bleed. Todd stands at the foot of his mother's bed to say good-bye. Jessica peeks in the room, then runs away. Todd goes after her.

"It's okay," the nurse says. "Most people don't want to stay with the body." We draw the sheet over Jeanne, bestowing modesty. One of her eyes has come open, so the nurse places a finger over Jeanne's eyelid and holds it for a moment.

"You were a good daughter," she says.

"Daughter-in-law," I correct.

"Is that right?" The nurse rolls the soiled pads into a bundle. "I truly thought you were her daughter."

Letter to the Lady of the House

Sometimes I feel like a motherless child
A long ways from home

Negro spiritual

I finally made myself walk into the hardware store and ask all the questions that told the salesperson I have no idea what I'm doing. You would have been proud of me, Jeanne.

I bought primer to block stains and seal odors and cover in one coat, the brushes and rollers and a new canvas drop cloth. I'm going to paint the bathroom where you smoked all those years. I've never painted an interior area, but as you used to say, it's good to try new things. You were always sure your kids could accomplish anything—and you extended that confidence to me when I became your daughter-in-law. Despite the struggles and tensions all those years, you always believed in me.

You limited your smoking to that one room, to spare the rest of the house the stench. Do you remember when you stopped smoking and I asked you if I could paint the bathroom? Oh, it reeked. I said you should have a fresh space, to celebrate quitting—but I confess thinking ahead to your death even then, when those walls, discolored and smelling of smoke, would need to be changed. But you said no, you didn't want to spend the money, and I let it go.

I don't think you knew how we all hated the stink from your cigarettes. I used to pull away from your hugs not because I was pulling away from you, but because of the smell of you: your breath, your clothes, even your skin. After you quit smoking, Todd confided to me that he still felt the urge to pull away when you drew close. He wasn't sure whether it was the cigarettes or the relationship that kept him at a distance all those years. I'm not sure he has worked this out, even now.

And I remember how you were troubled by the telltale lines left across your cheeks by the oxygen tubing. "I don't want anyone to know I use oxygen," you said. When Levearn came to visit after your first exacerbation, you told her the hospitalization was for a "massive chest infection of unknown cause." This sounded medical, but I knew you invented the "unknown cause" so you wouldn't have to say the word *emphysema*. When I walked Levearn to the door, she whispered to me, "Is Jeanne still smoking?" I stepped out past the door and closed it before I told her about the antianxiety meds and that I was sure you'd quit for good. I felt a twinge of guilt—but I couldn't lie to cover for your lies.

Later that day you seemed downhearted as you speculated about your dismal future. You made me promise never to make you go out in public once you needed oxygen full time. I pointed out to you that many people use oxygen, that there are small tanks you can carry in your tote bag. You didn't budge. I remember your words exactly: "It's embarrassing. People need oxygen for one reason only. I don't want to announce that to the world. I would rather just stay home."

You know all these things—you lived them, while I only observed. I'm reminding you because there's something more I want to say, and I will get to it soon, I promise. Oh, so many memories crowd in as I prepare to freshen this small bathroom of yours.

I've spread the drop cloth and have read up on technique. Your bathroom door is still white on the outside, but the years of smoke made the inside a dull apricot. Did you ever look at that color and wonder what the smoke was doing to your lungs?

❁

I used my new angled brush to paint the six raised panels and all the beveled parts around and between. The white paint over that apricot-colored door reminded me of the scene in *Charlotte's Web*, when Mrs. Zuckerman gives that pig a buttermilk bath. She puts on galoshes and a raincoat and climbs right into the pigpen, while Mr. Zuckerman watches in amazement. *I* painted barefoot. When I left too much paint on the brush, thick white drops trickled down the orange-pink door like buttermilk down Wilbur's side. It's the kind of thought I would have shared with you. The memory of your laugh pleased me as I painted.

My hand, used to typing and not brush strokes, became cramped and sore by the time I finished, but the door looked fresh. As the paint dried, peach ghosts materialized, limning the faux wood grain. One coat did not cover, despite the salesperson's pledge. And, Jeanne, I was angry with you—I *am* angry with you—because even now, after your death, your smoking still creates work for me.

Anger was a struggle for me these past few years. You saw me helping, serving, caring—everyone saw that and lauded me—but I hated how my life was tangled up with your needs, and I wanted out. You kept developing more conditions, more illnesses, until we were seeing doctors two and three times a week, and none of the treatments made a difference.

Shortly before you made the decision to receive comfort care from hospice, Todd and I had tickets for Shakespeare in the Park, over in Dallas. I'd taken you to see doctors three days that week, and I was afraid that you would need me to stay with you, as happened so much of the time near the end. But, Jeanne, I had to get away sometimes, to get out of the house for a while without pushing your wheelchair. Without *you*. I know this hurt your feelings, made you feel that I was abandoning you.

On the night I'm thinking of, I had asked Kathleen to come—a babysitter for the girls and company for you. Todd and I saw *The Merchant of Venice*. I know it well, having played Shylock's daughter, Jessica, twenty-six years ago at Oregon State. Todd and I settled into our camping chairs with a picnic dinner, and the sun dropped below the tree line behind the stage: *Enter Antonio, Salerio, and Solanio.* A young actor played Jessica, torn between her lover and her father. In that dusky Dallas park I whispered the lines along with her: "Alack, what heinous sin is it in me / To be asham'd to be my father's child!"

I memorized those lines as a college freshman, but twenty-five years ago I did not understand. They taught us method acting, but at eighteen and twenty we young actors didn't have much life experience to draw from. At forty-five, I'm probably too old to be cast as Jessica—but I understand her now. *Alack, what heinous sin is it in me / That I would long to see my mother-in-law's death.*

Oh, Jeanne, I hope you never knew. But there's something more I need to say to you, and I'm trying to find the right way to get there.

✿

The second coat went on beautifully and the door looks like new. I was so encouraged by my success that I taped the baseboards and started on the bathroom walls, which were oatmeal colored when we moved into the house. Your cigarette smoke made them the color of honey.

Jeanne, why didn't you let me do this for you years ago, when you quit? You had to stay in the body you ruined with cigarettes—but you could have had a fresh bathroom. Near the end, that room was only used by the aide when she emptied your catheter bag. The bathroom smelled so stale and strange that none of us wanted to enter it, so once you were bedfast we shut the door and kept it closed.

We're leaving Texas, Jeanne. I'm painting so we can sell this house, and soon. You always envisioned us living on here, as if this home were your legacy to us, but we have known for years that we would leave once you were gone. When you were sleeping those last weeks, in a morphine haze and finally pain free, Todd interviewed for a job in Oregon. The offer came two months after your death. We've had a real estate agent in to look around; she told me that before we could list the house I must paint your bathroom and erase all evidence that a smoker ever lived here.

I spend most of my days alone now—cleaning, painting, packing, writing—and I find myself thinking of more than just the tensions between us. I see how open and generous you were, Jeanne, how intimately you allowed me to know you, mind and body both. You stretched out your hand for mine, wanting to be reassured that you were loved. I took your hand but so often pulled quickly away, leaving you to feel rejected and useless. We continued stiffly, each of us trying imperfectly to do what was right. Oh, Jeanne, such hard steps we took together over the years. Such a sad and necessary dance.

✿

Your physical decline was so steep—looking back now I'm amazed that we didn't read the signs, and I wonder whether you ever did. When Dr. Fletcher instructed you to begin using oxygen full time, the skin around your lips was greenish blue and you couldn't walk from the waiting room to the exam room without huffing, but still you found breath to argue. That afternoon the rental company delivered tanks that fit in a shoulder tote, smaller and easier to manage than the large wheeled tanks we had tucked away beside your television cabinet. I didn't tell you this at the time, but I was so proud of how you named the little tanks "puffer bellies" and called them "cute" even though they must have pierced your pride so deeply. Yes, I was proud of you—but I still hated you for smoking all those years. You deprived yourself of the health you might have had in your seventies, and you deprived me of freedom I might have had in midlife. I'm glad I helped you through it, Jeanne, but I'm also so relieved that now it's over and, yes, I'm even relieved that you're gone.

The tubing trailed behind as you walked through the house, pulling it around corners and yanking at it when it seemed to be caught on something. You must have hated that tether, that leash. How sweetly you thanked me when I untangled it. I admired that, too, Jeanne, or at least I do now as I look back.

Do you remember your first trip out of the house wearing oxygen? We'd never seen anyone we knew in Costco, so it seemed like a good choice, and you made no mention of your earlier resolution. In the car I asked how you felt about going out in public with the oxygen for the first time.

"Embarrassed," you said. "It's hard to admit I'm frail."

You drove one of those motorized shopping scooters as I walked beside you with a large cart in the crowded store. Just ahead of us were three African American women, each with a cart, walking side by side and taking up nearly the entire width of the aisle. One of them stopped to look at a display, and her friends paused and waited for her, blocking our way. You put on the brakes and looked over at me with a big roll of your eyes, and in a gesture that said, *shame, shame on them,* you extended your left forefinger toward the women and made a motion like peeling a carrot. Before you could open your mouth, I turned my cart and hurried toward the back of the store. I thought you would be less tempted to make a mean-spirited comment about the slow shoppers if your primary audience was not by your side.

In the produce section I saw you again, across a wide table filled with flats of avocados and tomatoes. You were stuck again behind one of the slow shoppers. You looked my way and smiled a sweet smile, as if you had all the patience in the world as the tank puff-puffed at your side.

Looking at you, I saw once again how truly frail you had become. There would be no return to independence from oxygen, from electric carts and wheelchairs and walkers. You lifted a hand to me and waved with a grin.

My eyes filled with tears, so I pushed my cart to the end of the produce section and on down another aisle—to hide them. This is what I have been trying to tell you, Jeanne. I struggled for so long with frustration and resentment that I came to think any affection I displayed was a façade—the constant caregiver, the devoted daughter-in-law. But there I was, crying in Costco, and realizing that I loved you.

❁

I have not grieved much since your death. Maybe I did all my weeping in the years leading up to the end—tears over misunderstanding, over your needs, over the wife and mother I was not able to be because of caring for you. During the last month of your life, when hospice nurses came daily, I rarely cried. The hardest times were when you would say, "Why am I still here? What am I doing wrong? Shouldn't I be dead by now?" Yes, you had read the signs. I held your hand.

The day you died, they gathered up the four corners of your bed sheet like a disposable tablecloth after a party and lifted you onto the gurney. They zipped up the black bag and rolled you out of the house. Todd and I watched as they collapsed the legs of the gurney and lifted you into the van. They shut the doors and you were gone.

✤

I found boxes in the garage that were never unpacked during the seven years you lived with us. One of them held the hand-painted Dutch lamp you and your mother loved so well, the one with two farm girls wearing wooden shoes and aprons who stand tending goats in a meadow. In your home in Nebraska, the lamp had stood on a marble-topped table in your formal living room. I always liked the piece but never unpacked it for you because the girls were small and I was afraid to have something so valuable and fragile displayed in my home. But the girls are older now, so I unpacked the lamp and contacted an antiques expert, who told me it should be appraised and probably had value in the thousands.

Here's my confession. I had the lamp displayed in the front room, and a week ago we cleared things in preparation for the carpets to be steamed. When I lifted the lamp off the table, its globe toppled. My hands were full with the heavy bottom portion, or I might have been able to reach out and grab the globe, which fell to the carpet and shattered.

Todd came to help me clean up the broken glass. He knew about the value and asked, "How do you feel?"

"I feel absolutely free," I said, surprising myself. I didn't feel guilty at all. Things break. We gather the fragments and go on.

"You know, I bet Mom is laughing right now," Todd said.

I'm sure he was right! You passed this wonderful quality on to your sons—at least to the one I married. When something burns, when something breaks, when someone overspends, or misses an exit—Todd shrugs and laughs. I needed fifteen years of being married to him, maybe more, before I could let myself relax and, yes, *enjoy* myself when something goes wrong. This is a trait he takes from you, and I'm grateful.

✤

I've finished the bathroom now. No remaining odor of stale smoke or infected urine—just the peppery smell of fresh paint. I've been taping and mixing and rolling up a storm in the other rooms—striding confidently into the paint store whenever necessary to get exactly what I need. While

I'm painting, though, I still doubt myself, every time in every room. As the paint dries, it looks blotchy—dry and lighter in some areas, darker and somehow heavier where the paint is still wet. I have to resist the temptation to keep painting the same wall. If I can stand back—leave the room for a couple of hours—I return to smell the pepper scent and admire how the paint covers the stains and patches.

When the real estate agent first brought you and me here, the house was still under construction. Remember? We came to Texas while Todd stayed back in Pennsylvania, glad to avoid tromping through houses and analyzing the benefits of hardwood and granite. I remember how it felt, after a long day looking at houses not quite suitable for our extended family, to walk together through the door of this place and know we were home; I remember how you looked at me with eyebrows raised in pleasure.

"I think this is the one," I said.

"I believe it is, Lisa."

They hadn't laid the carpet yet—could it be the house was being painted when we first saw it? All this space, the many rooms and the private area toward the rear of the house for you—everything was perfect, right down to the fact that the home was trimmed with the dark woods that matched both your furniture and mine.

As executrix of your estate, I've passed along furniture, artwork, and precious knickknacks to all the family members and friends willing to take them. Your memory, as held in these belongings, lives now in nearly a dozen homes and hearts in varying geographies. The house here is feeling pleasantly sparse—good for showing to buyers, the agent says.

Mom, the time has come to close this letter. With my paintbrush and roller I have covered over the rubber marks from your walker and wheelchair, the evidence of your cigarettes, all the splashes and stains of our living together in this house.

I had rinsed the paintbrushes thoroughly before I realized that I could just throw them away. The next time I paint will be in Oregon, and I will buy a new set of supplies for my new home: I'll start fresh.

. I placed the usable painting supplies in a box for the thrift store, and nearly all the rest went into a heavy-duty black trash bag. The canvas drop cloth I'll keep, with its splotches of oatmeal and buttermilk paint.

Epilogue

On my right hand I now wear Jeanne's wedding ring. It's a pavé style with two rows of diamonds—twelve in all—set so closely together that they look like a sparkling mosaic, like a path paved of diamond cobblestones. Jeanne never took this ring off in her ten years of widowhood, not until the summer before she died, when her left hand became hot and tender and swollen and the ring began to grow tight. I helped her soap off the ring, and we placed it in a small, pink jewelry box on her bathroom counter for safekeeping.

When Jeanne's hand began to swell, her immunologist said it looked like a staph infection, hopefully not resistant, and he prescribed intravenous antibiotics. The treatment lasted six weeks before the immunologist shrugged at the lack of progress and sent us to a dermatologist instead. The swelling and soreness had gone down, but odd red bumps erupted into lesions on Jeanne's hand, wrist, and lower arm. The dermatologist said that the bumps weren't staph, that she could come back in four months if they hadn't cleared up. Jeanne began to receive hospice care just weeks after that appointment.

And now I wear her ring. I kept very few of Jeanne's things, but when Jeanne was dying I asked her if the ring could be mine. "I'd love for you to have it, dear," she said. After she was gone and I had the ring sized and cleaned, I was amazed at the fire in these diamonds. On her hand they had become dull and lifeless, like cut glass in a cheap cocktail ring. On my hand these stones are glorious.

In the final weeks of hospice care, Jeanne requested that we have her cremated. "Just bury me in a cardboard box," she said. "Those urns are too expensive." I assured her, there on her deathbed, that we would not bury her in a cardboard box.

"Don't worry, I won't spend too much," I said. Then a few weeks later I looked through a catalog of ugly brass boxes costing hundreds of dollars. The funeral director said, off the record, that any crockery with a lid would do nicely—a cookie jar, perhaps.

I spent a full morning shopping for Jeanne's urn, unable to make a decision. All those years of shopping together for handbags, for gifts, for a new clock, for pillows, a bedspread: I knew what Jeanne liked. She liked things brightly colored and ornate. Throw some sparkle in and she was doubly pleased. I dressed mostly in blacks and browns and decorated the main areas of our shared home in earth tones: cranberry and taupe and dark wood to Jeanne's pink and blue in-law suite, its walls crowded with decorative plates and paintings in gilded frames.

I lined up urns along the edge of the store shelf to try and decide. The tallest was something Jeanne would have loved: a Royal Delft–looking blue and white. I was more drawn to the urn I set next on the shelf—a swooping design of matte black on a polished black urn, subtle and classy and very much *my* taste rather than Jeanne's. What if I chose an urn that all her sons hated? Or what if I betrayed Jeanne somehow by choosing *my* taste for her burial wear? With my cell phone I snapped pictures and sent them to Todd and Jeff. Todd immediately texted back, "Looks great," but I didn't hear from Jeff. I walked the aisles of the store with two urns in my cart, wondering if I might happen on a third, more perfect, choice. Still no text from Jeff. Finally, knowing what Jeanne would have chosen, I bought the blue urn. *Who cares?* I said to myself. *It'll be buried.* Jeff finally texted back while I was driving to the funeral home to deliver the urn: "Lisa, I love you. Whatever you get is fine."

The closer I got to the funeral home, the more I felt like the Delft blue really was a cookie jar. It stood nearly twenty inches high, and I felt a bit embarrassed handing it over to be filled. I reminded myself how much Jeanne would have loved this pattern.

The blue urn was too big for her "cremains." How was I to guess what volume of ashes an overweight old woman would burn down to? The ashes would rattle in such a tall urn, the funeral guy said, and we would need a much deeper hole dug to accommodate it. With this news, the decision was easy. I returned the Delft cookie jar in exchange for the black urn. I felt peace even before Jeff told me he really thought the blue looked like an old lady's kitchen décor and he liked the black much better. What do the dead care? I hope Jeanne had a good laugh over my troubles shopping without her. I know she would have loved the idea of being buried in a cookie jar.

There are other ways in which Jeanne and I were a misfit pair, of course. But in the end I sat at her memorial service and thought, *I did it. I didn't screw up. I didn't send her to a nursing home. I kept on until the end, and I was good to her.* I didn't finish perfectly, but I finished well. And I loved my mother-in-law. I do not miss her the way I read of people missing loved ones. I don't catch a whiff of her perfume and long for her touch. The memories I have of Jeanne are too hard, too intimate. I can still feel the spongy heat of her infected skin, the greenish color of her sputum that signaled another pneumonia, the cough that sounded like her lungs were being torn with each spasm. I remember too easily the hurtful words, the silent treatment, the disguised criticisms.

But there were moments. Times when I did feel compassion, when it didn't matter that she had done this to herself over many years of smoking. When the nurses probed after veins grown too thin, when Jeanne clenched her teeth and closed her eyes to endure the pain as a team of nurses tried to clear a blockage in her chest port. Too many times in those last months I watched Jeanne subject herself to painful procedures at the hands, or directives, of doctors who knew she had no hope of getting better. She always said once she knew she was at the end of her life, she would not fight; she did not want to extend the pain. Knowing that, and knowing how much pain she endured unnecessarily, I grieve. We didn't know the right questions to ask, the right ways to communicate with her doctors so they would understand. Jeanne filled out all the forms and knew that at the end of her life she wanted peace, and she wanted to be at home. But we didn't know how to recognize when the end of life was near. And the doctors, those who could see clearly, did not tell us.

During a break in the Oregon rain I put on garden gloves and go outside to pull weeds. The early crocuses are soft and wilting, but the daffodils—my favorite—are now blooming. All around me the world is fresh and bright.

For all my anxiety over tornado watches and warnings, I miss the stampeding storms of a Texas spring. Thunderstorms are often dangerous, but approaching heavy clouds are visible for miles across that flat landscape. Take in the yard furniture and toys that will become projectiles in the strong wind. Move the car into the garage to avoid hail damage. Close the windows against wind and rain, and put fresh batteries in the weather radio, just in case the sirens wail and you must seek shelter.

I've been gone long enough that it's hard to recall the sheer quantity of rain that fell in thirty minutes, sending a river of drainage through our side yard. I used to measure each storm by how close our street came to completely filling with water.

In this new season of life I find the rains are gentler, and I keep at my yard work even as the rain mists, then lets up. Our home backs to an acre or so of fir trees and maples sloping down to several more acres of a shared neighborhood greenway along the brambled creek. My girls are free to wander. The other day Laurie came back from her solitary hike to tell me she'd recited a poem right out loud, with good projection, because she knew no one was close enough to hear.

When I place my yard trimmings into the compost bin, I see how the blackberry vines are already taking over the side stairs. I find my leather gloves and make multiple trips to the compost bin, gingerly balancing an armload of brambles each time. Next to the blackberries, the rosemary is overgrown. I have no idea what time of year I should be cutting back rosemary, but I have a feeling it doesn't matter. I cut boldly, knowing that these darlings will all grow back soon enough. No worries about trimming too much. I cut great handfuls of rosemary until my hands and hair smell like an Easter feast.

I miss Jeanne. I do. We've started a new life in a beautiful place because Jeanne died and released me from caregiving. Now instead of learning side effects to medications, I am memorizing the names of the trees and mountain ranges and the April flowers springing up in my garden.

I've just pulled off my gloves and am brushing damp soil from the knees of my jeans when I hear geese. I tilt my head up and raise a hand to shield myself from the rain as I peer into the sky and see the flock overhead, winging and honking and flying free to their summer home.

Index

About the Author

Lisa Ohlen Harris lives in northwest Oregon with her husband and four daughters. She is the author of the Middle East memoir *Through the Veil*, a 2011 finalist for the Oregon Book Award. www.lisaohlenharris.com